Playwrights for Tomorrow

VOLUME 2

Tango Palace

BY MARIA IRENE FORNÉS

The Successful Life of Three

BY MARIA IRENE FORNÉS

Shelter Area

BY NICK BORETZ

. . . And the Boy Who Came to Leave

BY LEE H. KALCHEIM

EDITED, WITH AN INTRODUCTION, BY ARTHUR H. BALLET

PLAYWRIGHTS FOR TOMORROW

A Collection of Plays, Volume 2

THE UNIVERSITY OF MINNESOTA PRESS · MINNEAPOLIS

Printed in the United States of America at the North Central Publishing Company, St. Paul

Library of Congress Catalog Card Number: 66-19124

PUBLISHED IN GREAT BRITAIN, INDIA, AND PAKISTAN BY THE OXFORD UNIVERSITY PRESS, LONDON, BOMBAY, AND KARACHI, AND IN CANADA BY THE COPP CLARK PUBLISHING CO. LIMITED, TORONTO

Playwrights for Tomorrow

VOLUME 2

PLAYWRIGHTS FOR TOMORROW

Arthur H. Ballet

O F THE artists who band together to share the theatrical experience, the playwright's lot is the loneliest and perhaps the most difficult. In modern America, he generally writes in a vacuum, deprived of colleagues, of intellectual stimulation, and of meaningful theatrical contact.

This isolation of the writer is disastrous. Historically, the important contributions to theatre have come from writers who were intimately involved as artists and as people with a specific theatre or at least with an individual school of ideas and practice.

The plight of the new writer is especially critical. There is ample assurance that he can, alone at his typewriter, turn out a script. But unless he can then work within that creative bond of writer, director, actor, and audience which results in a living play, his talent will not be developed, his potential will remain unrealized. He must be allowed to try this and then that, to rework and start afresh. Yet he is engaging in an art that, in the present day, does not permit failure, whose audience judges each aspiring effort with finality. What is desperately needed is the opportunity for many writers to have their work for the theatre tried out, developed, viewed, and evaluated. Only in this way can we hope for a vital, relevant theatre.

Once the commercial theatre and local repertory companies could and did chance it with new writers. Today, costs are prohibitive in the commercial theatre, local repertory is turning more and more to "safe classics," and university and collegiate theatres are too frequently bent on emulating commercial success. There is no room for the experimental writer, for the beginner who might *learn* to be a good playwright.

3

In foolhardy fashion, fresh theatre in this country has survived in a single city, New York. Here new plays are welcomed and given their hour upon the stage — albeit dogged by struggles with standards set by the countinghouse, audiences who seek solely to be diverted, unions which are preserving a battle station of protectivity long outdated, and artists who are self-centered rather than art-centered. The miracle is that any new play is ever produced in this bedlam, let alone that significant new drama can emerge. Nonetheless, it has been the New York theatre, and, regrettably, the New York theatre almost alone, which has had the courage to present new playwrights, to experiment with form and meaning, and to underwrite changes in the status quo.

The provincial theatre has for the most part been precisely that: provincial, either sacrosanctly re-presenting the "classics" of a foreign heritage or righteously bringing to the hinterlands rehashes of the Broadway and off-Broadway success. Instead of providing the lifeblood of the so-called commercial theatre, educational and community theatres too often have bled it. Despite elegantly equipped playhouses and well-attended productions, they have failed to venture very far afield and consequently are insignificant except as rerun houses. Secure in their audiences and successes, they have retreated from artistic honesty and experimentation with the lament that "the audiences will not accept new plays." They refuse to recognize that the only important theatre in the country, that which is in New York, has survived — haphazardly to be sure — *only* on new plays.

At the same time, dramatists by the hundreds have gone unproduced, unseen, and unheard because they do not measure up to a New York producer's estimate of what will "go." And the producer is not to be blamed for his judgment; his risk will be enormous and he must rely, however mistakenly, on his own taste and estimate of what will work and what will not. Simultaneously, the writer lucky enough to get a New York hearing risks his whole career in that single hearing, for the unreasonable and catastrophic alternatives of smash hit or utter failure face him — and both success and failure on the gargantuan scale of Broadway are too frequently catastrophic for the new writer as a creative artist. There is no in-between, no chance to consider his work in terms of a company of actors, a theatre, and a community, no chance to rewrite on the basis of audience and player reactions. At best, a play is produced; it is seldom developed.

In an attempt to help remedy this bleak situation, the University of Minnesota, in 1963, undertook an experiment with the aid and encouragement of the Rockefeller Foundation. An Office for Advanced Drama Research (O.A.D.R.) was set up with the charge of exploring what helpful relationships might be established between professional playwrights and a thriving center of theatre activity outside of New York City. In the Twin Cities of Minneapolis and St. Paul, there were the Tyrone Guthrie Theatre, the University of Minnesota Theatre, Theatre in the Round Players, Theatre St. Paul, and the Firehouse Theatre — each theatrically knowledgeable and each representative of a variety of dramatic experience. These theatres, together with some twenty other local groups, many equally dedicated and skilled, formed a nucleus on which the O.A.D.R. could rely for support. It is hoped that, in time, most of these theatres, whether professional, semiprofessional, or amateur, will be involved in producing new writers.

University of Minnesota President O. Meredith Wilson named an Executive Committee for the project: Donald K. Smith, assistant academic vice-president of the University of Minnesota, chairman; Oliver Rea and Peter Zeisler, co-managing directors of the Minnesota Theatre Company at the Guthrie Theatre; Willard T. Thompson, dean of the Extension Division of the university; Frank M. Whiting, director of the University Theatre; and Kenneth L. Graham, chairman of the university's Speech and Theatre Arts Department.

As director of the O.A.D.R., I began by asking established theatre people for recommendations of promising young playwrights and then invited submission of scripts from them. Word got around, and other plays began to pour in. All the literally hundreds of manuscripts submitted each year were read carefully. Insofar as possible, the selection of participants was based on their talent for dramatic writing — potential if not always fully realized — and for generating what I can best describe as theatrical excitement. In no case was a *play* selected; my sole concern was the *playwright*. Once chosen, the writer was given the widest possible latitude. He was encouraged to explore his own dramatic efforts freely and honestly, without external pressures. One writer chose to direct her own play; another chose to observe a professional company at work and to perfect, rewrite, and create new plays. With one exception, when a cast and a director were experimentally "imported" from New York, the

5

writers worked with local companies and directors. The plays were circulated to the cooperating theatres, which were free to accept or reject the scripts in terms of their own theatrical goals. Each play developmentally rehearsed under the auspices of the O.A.D.R. was viewed not only by an adequate cross-sampling of local theatregoers, but by guest critics, directors, and actors, brought to the Twin Cities at the playwright's request to help him evaluate his work.

The plays need now to be examined by a wider audience. To that end they are being published in book form. Seven of the first eight playwrights invited to avail themselves of the facilities of the program are represented here and in Volume 1 of *Playwrights for Tomorrow*. (One writer did not wish to have his play published.) The play that concludes Volume 1 — *And Things That Go Bump in the Night* — has already been seen in New York; the published criticism of the play was damning, but the reader, and I sincerely hope other audiences, will judge independently. The newest work of Megan Terry, another of the playwrights represented in Volume 1, has been optioned for 1966 production on Broadway. Since working with the O.A.D.R. on the two one-act plays that appear in this volume, Maria Irene Fornés has been given the Obie Award as the outstanding new writer on the 1964 off-Broadway scene, and she is preparing for the production of another of her plays in New York. Each of the playwrights, in short, continues to write and to work productively in the theatre.

The writers were invited to comment on their plays and their experiences with the O.A.D.R., and each has responded in his own way. Their remarks are included here as prefatory notes to the plays.

For the reader who seeks in these plays a connecting thread of commitment, there will be disappointment. They range in theme and subject matter from cosmic apocalypse through social misalliance to personal inadequacy. Some are mature and wise, while others are young and angry. If they share anything it is simply that each represents, I believe, a new and exciting voice in the American theatre.

MARIA IRENE FORNÉS

Two One-Act Plays

Tango Palace and *The Successful Life of Three* by Maria Irene Fornés were presented on January 14, 15, 16, 22, 23, 28, 29, 30 and on February 4, 5, 6, 1965, at the Firehouse Theatre, Minneapolis.

    Tango Palace was directed by Charles M. Morrison; *The Successful Life of Three* was directed by Miss Fornés.

Cast of Characters for TANGO PALACE

ISIDORE	Lionel Reid
LEOPOLD	Michael Devine

Cast of Characters for THE SUCCESSFUL LIFE OF THREE

HE	Jeff Moses
SHE	Carrie Bartlett
THREE	Mel Semler

PLAYWRIGHT'S PREFACE

To say that a work of art is meaningful is to imply that the work is endowed with intelligence. That it is illuminating. But if we must inquire what the meaning of a work of art is, it becomes evident that the work has failed us; that we have not been inspired by it; that the work has not succeeded in breathing its life for us.

To approach a work of art with the wish to decipher its symbolism, and to extract the author's intentions from it, is to imply that the work can be something other than what it demonstrates, that the work can be treated as a code system which, when deciphered, reveals the true content of the work. A work of art should not be other than what it demonstrates. It should not be an intellectual puzzle, or at least not primarily. A true work of art is a magic thing. To comprehend magic we must be in a state of innocence, of credulity. If there is wisdom in the work it will come to us. But if we go after it, we become wary, watchful. We lose our ability to taste.

A work of art must have its function, like a car, a window, or a bridge. We all know how a car, or a window, or a bridge must function. We know whether the designer or engineer has succeeded. However, we are not too sure how art must function. Art must inspire us. That is its function.

If art is to inspire us, we must not be too eager to understand. If we understand too readily, our understanding will, most likely, be meaningless. It will have no consequences. We must be patient with ourselves.

We have learned to think of inspiration as the property of artists. It is not. Inspiration belongs to all of us. What the artist does with his inspiration is quite clear. He creates his work of art. The product of his inspiration becomes public. The inspiration of the layman generates itself in his personal life. It enriches it, and ennobles it. Inspiration is a precious gift which we have relinquished without any struggle. We do not believe that it belongs to us.

Art is created by the artist for the layman. The layman must take possession of it. He must become familiar with it. He must make himself worthy of being its judge. He must love it.

I give my most sincere thanks to the John Hay Whitney Foundation for awarding me an Opportunity Fellowship in 1961 to write *Tango Palace* and to Herbert Blau and the San Francisco Actor's Workshop for its first production on November 29, 1963. I wish also to express my deep appreciation to Arthur Ballet and the Office for Advanced Drama Research and to Charles M. Morrison III and Marlow Hotchiss of the Firehouse Theatre for making possible the first production of *The Successful Life of Three*, along with a production of the revised version of *Tango Palace*, at the Firehouse Theatre on January 15, 1965.

MARIA IRENE FORNÉS

New York City
July 1965

TANGO PALACE

Cast of Characters

ISIDORE, an androgynous clown
LEOPOLD, an earnest youth

The Scene

A room, the same throughout the play. The floor is carpeted. The door is bolted with an oversize padlock. There is a big filing cabinet, an armchair, a secretary, a wall mirror, a water jug, a radio, three porcelain teapots, a large vase, a blackboard. There is a large canvas sack on the floor. A recess in the back wall serves as a shrine. Within the recess, hanging from nails, are a guitar, a whip, a toy parrot, a Persian helmet, two swords, a cape, a compass, a muleta, a pair of bulls horns, six banderillas, two masks in the form of beetles' faces. The shrine is decorated with a string of flower-shaped light bulbs. Isidore sits in the shrine. His appearance is a mixture of man and woman. He is stout, has long hair, and is wearing rouge and lipstick; he wears a man's hat and pants, high-heeled shoes, and a silk shirt. There is a corsage of flowers pinned on his shirt. Sometimes his behavior is clearly masculine; other times he could be thought a woman. Leopold is inside the canvas sack. He is in his late twenties. He is handsome, and his movements are simple. He wears a business suit. Each time Isidore feels he has said something important, he takes a card from his pocket or from a drawer and flips it across the room in any direction. (The word "card" in the script indicates when a card should be flipped.) This action is automatic.

TANGO PALACE

SCENE 1

Isidore makes a gesture and his shrine is lit. He makes another gesture and chimes sound. One more gesture and the bulbs on his shrine light up. Leopold begins to move inside the canvas sack. Isidore notices the sack and cautiously approaches it.

ISIDORE

Look what the stork has brought me. (*Isidore opens the sack. Leopold begins to emerge. They stare at each other for a while. Isidore is delighted with what he has found. He goes to the shrine, takes the guitar and begins to sing "A Sleepy Lagoon" in an attempt to charm Leopold.*) Song and guitar accompaniment by Isidore. (*card*) (*Leopold has gotten out of the sack and walks curiously about the room. He stops in front of the armchair. Isidore, noticing Leopold's interest in the furniture, addresses him in the affected tones of a salesman in an exclusive shop.*) Queen Anne walnut armchair. Representing the acme of artistic craftsmanship of the Philadelphia school. Circa 1740. Original condition and finish. (*card*) (*Isidore steps down from the shrine, walks ostentatiously past Leopold, and runs his hand along the surface of the secretary*) Very rare, small, Louis Quinze secretary, representing the acme of artistic craftsmanship of the Parisian school. A pure Louis Quinze leg was never, under any conditions, straight. It was always curvilinear, generally in that shaping which we have come to know as the "cabriole." (*card*) (*taking little steps to the mirror*) Louis Quatorze carved and gilded mirror. (*card*) Bearing sprays of leafage and flowers. Circa 1700. Height sixty-four inches. Width thirty-six inches. (*Isidore walks close to Leo-*

pold and looks him over) The choice of the examples here is influenced by their significance as distinct types representative of the best tradition, not only in the style and execution but in the choice of subject. (*card*) (*Isidore walks toward the shelf containing the porcelain objects*) Teapots of rarest Chinese export porcelain with American marine decoration. Circa 1740–1750. Left one shows American flag, right one American admiral's insignia. The one in the center depicts the so-called "Governor Duff," actually Diedrick Durven, governor general of the Dutch East India Company. Exquisite, isn't it? This collection has been formed throughout a period of many years, and it is probably not an exaggeration to say that such a collection could not be formed again. (*Isidore waits for a reaction*) Did you say something? . . Oh, well . . Listen . . Music . . A tango . . (*card*) (*Isidore begins to dance*) Do you know this step? Stomach in. Derrière out. Fingers gracefully curved. (*card*) A smile on your lips. Eyes full of stars. Dancing has well been called the poetry of motion. It is the art whereby the feelings of the mind are expressed by measured steps, regulated motions of the body, and graceful gestures. The German waltz, the Spanish fandango, the Polish mazurka, and last but not least the Argentine tango. One . . two . . three . . dip and turn your head to show your profile. One . . two . . three . . dip and swing your little foot back and forth. (*Leopold begins to imitate Isidore*) One . . two . . three . . and rotate on one foot, taking little steps with the other. Watch me first. Now you made me lose my step. And a one and a two and a three. Stomach in. Derrière out. Fingers gracefully curved. A smile on your lips. Eyes full of stars. One . . two . . three . . dip and profile. One . . two . . three . . dip and swing your little foot. One . . two . . three . . and rotate. (*Leopold's attention is drawn by the shrine; he moves closer to it*) Don't look there yet. Watch me . . watch me. (*Leopold watches for a moment, then he turns to the shrine again and reaches for the whip. Isidore takes the whip and demonstrates its use.*) This is my whip. (*lashing Leopold*) And that is pain. (*card*) A souvenir of love. I loved her. She loved me. I gave her the whip. She gave me her cherry . . All is fair in love and war. (*card*) (*taking the parrot*) This is my talking parrot. (*to the parrot*) Pretty parrot.

PARROT

Pretty parrot.

ISIDORE

Very smart. He knows everything.

PARROT

Very smart. He knows everything.

ISIDORE

Thank you.

PARROT

Thank you.

ISIDORE

(*putting on the Persian helmet*) And this is the genuine Persian helmet I wore when I fought in Salamis. (*card*) I killed two hundred and fifteen Athenians. Fourteen were captains, three were generals, and the rest foot soldiers. I'll show you. (*Isidore takes the sword and swings it while he screams, grunts, whirls, and hops. Leopold becomes frightened.*) That's how I killed them. Don't be afraid, I won't hurt you. (*touching Leopold's chest with the tip of the sword*) Do you have something to show me?

LEOPOLD

No. I don't have anything.

ISIDORE

Nothing at all?

LEOPOLD

No.

ISIDORE

Oh, that's too bad. Here, I'll show you my flying cape. (*Isidore puts on the cape, climbs on a chair, flips his arms, and jumps to the floor*) Extraordinary, isn't it? Would you like to see my joy compass? (*showing joy compass*) It's magic. I sent for it . . It points to joy. Now you show me something.

LEOPOLD

I don't own anything.

ISIDORE

Were your things taken away?

LEOPOLD

No, I never had anything, except . .

ISIDORE

What?

LEOPOLD

A tattoo. (*Leopold opens his shirt*)

ISIDORE

Oh. How beautiful. (*reading*) "This is man. Heaven or bust." Oh, that's in bad taste. That's in terrible taste. (*card*) Just for that you can't touch any of my things. The only things you can touch are those cards. Those cards are yours. (*card*)

LEOPOLD

(*picking up a card*) These cards are mine? (*reading*) "A tattoo." "Oh. How beautiful. This is man. Heaven or bust. Oh, that's in bad taste."

ISIDORE

You can put them there in that filing cabinet.

LEOPOLD

(*disturbed*) Why do you write what I say?

ISIDORE

First of all, I write what *we* say. And then I don't write, I print . . with my magic printing press . . if you'd like to know. File them in your filing cabinet. That cabinet is yours too.

LEOPOLD

What for?

ISIDORE

So you can find them when you need them. These cards contain wisdom. File them away. (*card*) Know where they are. (*card*) Have them at hand. (*card*) Be one upon whom nothing is lost. (*card*) Memorize them and you'll be where you were. (*card*) Be where you are. Then and now. Pick them up.

LEOPOLD

(*reading a card*) "All is fair in love and war."

ISIDORE

That's a good one.

LEOPOLD

Why?

ISIDORE

Because it teaches you that all is fair in love and war, and it teaches you that when someone is telling you a story about love and war, you are not to stand there and say . . That's not fair . . or you'll be considered a perfect fool. (*card*)

LEOPOLD

(*still disturbed*) I don't see why love in war should be different from love in anything else.

ISIDORE

(*pulling Leopold's ear and shouting*) Not love *in* war. Love *and* war! It has taken centuries . . (*smack*) centuries, to arrive at this ethical insight and you say it isn't fair. (*smack*) All is fair. You hear? All is fair in love . . (*smack*) and war. (*smack*)

LEOPOLD

I don't want your cards. I don't want to have anything to do with them.

ISIDORE

These are not my cards. They are yours. It's you who need learning, not me. I've learned already. (*card*) I know all my cards by heart. (*card*) And I have never forgotten one of them. (*card*) I can recite them in chronological order and I don't leave one word out. (*card*) What's more I never say a thing which is not an exact quotation from one of my cards. (*card*) That's why I never hesitate. (*card*) I'm never short of an answer. (*card*) Or a question. (*card*) Or a remark (*card*) if a remark is more appropriate.

LEOPOLD

I don't want to learn that way.

ISIDORE

There is no other way.

LEOPOLD

Yes, there is. I hear a voice.

ISIDORE

What voice? That's me you hear. I am the only voice.

LEOPOLD

No, it's not you.

ISIDORE

It is so. (*in a falsetto voice*) Listen to me and always obey me . . It's me . . me . . It's me . . and only me . . Leopold . . Lippy . . me . . me . .

LEOPOLD

No.

ISIDORE

Well, *Dime con quien andas y te dire quien eres* . . (*card*) Spanish proverb meaning . . You know what it means, and if you don't, go and ask that voice of yours . . What does your voice say?

LEOPOLD

You speak like a parrot.

ISIDORE

No, I don't. (*Isidore considers for a moment*) My diction is better. Sally says she sells sea shells at the seashore. Have you ever heard a parrot say: Sally says she sells sea shells at the seashore?

LEOPOLD

That's not what I mean. (*Isidore considers for a moment*)

ISIDORE

I talk like a wise parrot. Study hard, learn your cards, and one day you too will be able to talk like a parrot.

LEOPOLD

(*imitating a parrot*) Study hard, learn your cards, and one day you too will be able to talk like a parrot.

ISIDORE

What are you, a parrot? Do you want to be a moron for the rest of your life? Always being pushed around? (*Isidore pushes Leopold*) Are you mentally retarded? Do I have to tell you what should be obvious to a half-wit. (*smack*) It should be obvious (*smack*) even (*smack*) to a half-wit. (*Leopold throws a punch at Isidore. Isidore ducks, and kicks Leopold. Leopold falls. Isidore turns and thrusts his buttocks out.*) You bad, bad boy. You'll have to be punished. You tried to hit your loving teacher. Come. (*Isidore picks Leopold up*)

LEOPOLD

(*freeing himself from Isidore*) Take your hands off me. (*Leopold executes each of Isidore's commands at the same time as they are spoken, but as if he were acting spontaneously rather than obeying*)

ISIDORE

Walk to the door. (*card*) Notice the padlock. (*card*) Push the door. (*card*) You're locked in. (*card*) Stand there and think. (*card*) Why are you locked in? (*card*) Where are you locked in? (*card*) Turn to the door. (*card*) You know what to do. (*card*) Pull the padlock. (*card*) Push the door. (*card*) Force the padlock. (*card*) You are locked in. (*card*) Kick the door. (*card*) Bang the door. (*card*) Scream.

ISIDORE AND LEOPOLD

Anybody there! Anybody there! (*card*) Let me out. (*card*) Open up! (*card*)

ISIDORE

Kick the door. (*card*) Walk around the room restlessly. (*card*) Bite your thumbnails. (*card*) Get an idea. (*card*) You got an idea. (*card*) (*Leopold charges toward Isidore*) Violence does not pay. (*card*) Be sensible, stand still a moment being sensible. Have sensible thought. For every door there's a key. (*card*) The key must be in the room. Look for it in the obvious place first. Under the rare seventeenth-century needlework carpet depicting Elijah in the desert fed by ravens. It's not there. Look in Louis Quinze secretary, mahogany wood. Look in less obvious places. Magnificent marked Wedgwood vase in Rosso Antico ground. In flyleaf of my Gutenberg Bible. Look in places which are not obvious at all. Correction. All places are obvious places. (*card*) Look again in drawer of very rare, small, Louis Quinze secretary, representing the acme of artistic craftsmanship. Fall exhausted on Queen Anne chair. Have desperate thoughts.

18

(*Leopold kicks the chair. Isidore speaks soothingly, to regain control.*)
Collect yourself, darling. You must collect yourself.

LEOPOLD

I must collect myself.

ISIDORE

You must collect yourself. You must think, dear. Let's think. Could you
have enemies? Perhaps business associates? Perhaps people who envy
you? Or could it be the others? The angry husbands? The spinsters? The
barking dogs? The man whose toilet you dirtied?

LEOPOLD

Could it be you?

ISIDORE

Could it be you? It doesn't really matter. You might as well stay. Just tidy
up your things, darling. Do as I said. File them away. (*Leopold picks up
a card and reads it*)

LEOPOLD

And that is pain.

ISIDORE

Be where you were. (*card*)

LEOPOLD

(*reading another card*) Pretty parrot. Very smart. He knows everything.

ISIDORE

Then and now. (*card*)

LEOPOLD

(*reading another card*) Were your things taken away?

ISIDORE

Nothing is lost. (*card*)

LEOPOLD

Nothing is lost?

ISIDORE

Nothing. Come, it's time for your drawing lesson. (*Isidore rings the bell
and walks to the blackboard to illustrate the lesson*) How to draw a portrait. (*making a mark at the top of the blackboard*) This is the divine.
Cleopatra for example. (*making a mark at the bottom of the blackboard*)
This down here is the despicable. The werewolf. Now we're going to place
the person whose portrait we're drawing. Where shall we put him? Close
to the divine? Not so close. Halfway down? Close to the despicable? No.
Here. (*Isidore makes a mark to the left and halfway between the other
two marks*) Now you join the points with lines. This is the portrait of a

19

mediocre person. You can draw a mouth on it. And an eye. But it isn't necessary. Because what counts is the nose.

The figure Isidore has drawn looks like this:

LEOPOLD

Draw my portrait.

ISIDORE

Unfortunately this system doesn't do you any good, since all we can establish is that I am at the top. And way down at the bottom is you. There is no other point. We therefore can't have an angle. We only have a vertical line. The space around us is infinite, enclosed as it may be, because there is not a third person. And if the space around us is infinite, so is, necessarily, the space between us.

LEOPOLD

Who says you're at the top?

ISIDORE

I.

LEOPOLD

I say you're not at the top.

ISIDORE

But I am.

LEOPOLD

How do you know?

ISIDORE

Because I know everything. I know my cards. I know everything.

LEOPOLD

I'm going to burn those cards.

ISIDORE

You'll die if you burn them . . Don't take my word for it. Try it. (*Leopold sets fire to a card*) What in the world are you doing? Are you crazy? (*Isidore puts the fire out*) Are you out of your mind? You're going to die. Are you dying? Do you feel awful? (*Isidore trips Leopold*) There! You died.

LEOPOLD

(*springing to his feet*) No, I tripped. I think I tripped.

ISIDORE

See? You tripped because you burned that card. If I hadn't put the fire out you would have died.

LEOPOLD

I don't believe you.

ISIDORE

You don't believe me? You could have broken your neck. All right, I don't care what you think. You just stop burning things.

LEOPOLD

You're lying to me, aren't you?

ISIDORE

Go on, burn them if you want to. I won't stop you. (*Leopold moves to burn a card but then stops himself. Isidore flips a card at Leopold.*) Wisdom. (*card*) (*Isidore begins to dance*)

LEOPOLD

(*holding Isidore to stop him from dancing*) I beg you.

ISIDORE

Don't put your hands on me, ever, ever, ever, *ari, ari, ari.* That's Bengali, you know. (*card*) It's you who need learning. (*card*) Very smart. He knows everything. (*card*) A souvenir of love. She gave me her cherry. (*card*) I killed two hundred and fifteen Athenians. (*card*) That's a good one. (*card*) A sleepy lagoon. (*card*) What does your voice say? (*card*)

LEOPOLD

Stop flipping those things at me . . I beg you . . Don't . . Please . . I beg you. (*kneels at Isidore's feet*)

ISIDORE

And a one and a two. One, two, three, dip and turn . . You still have to be punished. Don't think I forgot. (*Isidore takes Leopold by the hand and walks him to a corner. Leopold leans against the wall.*) Straighten yourself up. Are you hearing things again? I'm jealous. I want to hear too. (*putting his ear against Leopold's ear*) Where is it? I can't hear a thing. (*talking into Leopold's ear*) Yoo hoo. Where are you? Say something. Talk to me. It won't talk to me. (*to Leopold*) Tell me what it says. I'm angry. (*Isidore sits on the shrine, crosses his legs and his arms, and turns his head away from Leopold*) I'm angry. Don't talk to me. I said don't talk to me. Don't you see I'm in the typical position of anger? . . Do you want to say something to me?

LEOPOLD

No.

ISIDORE

Well, I want you to tell me what that awful voice was telling you.

LEOPOLD

It said, "Isidore deceives you." It said, "Don't listen to Isidore."

ISIDORE

Oh. Horrible. Horrible. Treason in my own house.

LEOPOLD
Let me tell you . .

ISIDORE
Oh. Don't say any more, treason. Oh.

LEOPOLD
Let me tell you what I think, Isidore.

ISIDORE
No.

LEOPOLD
Please.

ISIDORE
You've said enough.

LEOPOLD
I haven't said . .

ISIDORE
Treason!

LEOPOLD
Isidore!

ISIDORE
(*in a whisper*) Don't talk so loud.

LEOPOLD
(*in a whisper*) I haven't said . .

ISIDORE
I heard you already. Treason!

LEOPOLD
I want to leave.

ISIDORE
Bye, bye, butterfly.

LEOPOLD
I want to get out.

ISIDORE
See you later, alligator.

LEOPOLD
Give me the key.

ISIDORE
Pretty parrot.

PARROT
Pretty parrot.

LEOPOLD
I want the key.

ISIDORE
He wants the key.
PARROT
He wants the key.
ISIDORE
There is no key.
PARROT
No key.
LEOPOLD
You're lying.
ISIDORE
I always tell the truth. I worship truth and truth worships me. Don't be so stubborn. There is no key.
LEOPOLD
There must be a key.
ISIDORE
I see what possesses you. It's faith!
LEOPOLD
So what?
ISIDORE
Faith is a disgusting thing. It's treacherous and destructive. Mountains are moved from place to place. You can't find them. I won't have any of that.
LEOPOLD
Well, I do have faith.
ISIDORE
Infidel. I'm too upset. I can't take any more of this. (*covering his face*) It's the devil. I can't look at you. Tell me you'll give it up. Tell me you have no faith.
LEOPOLD
But I do.
ISIDORE
Well, I'm a mountain. *Move me.*
LEOPOLD
I know there is a way out because there have been moments when I have been away from here.
ISIDORE
That's not true. You get ten demerits for telling lies.
LEOPOLD
It is true. There are moments when you have just vanished . .

23

ISIDORE

Vanished? I have never vanished.

LEOPOLD

I don't mean vanished . . exactly . . I mean there are moments when I've felt this is not all there is.

ISIDORE

What else is there?

LEOPOLD

Close your eyes . . Imagine . . that all is calm.

ISIDORE

I don't like playing childish games. I'm supposed to sit there imagining a field of orange blossoms and then you're going to pour a bucket of water on my head. Let me tell you, young man, that I played that game when I was five. Let me tell you that it was I who invented that game. And let me tell you that I didn't invent it to sit there like a fool and get the water on *my* head. I invented it to pour the water on the fool's head. Let me tell you that. You're not smart enough . . not for old Izzy. (*card*)

LEOPOLD

I wasn't going to throw water on you.

ISIDORE

You weren't? Hm . . All right. Go on.

LEOPOLD

Don't imagine anything in particular. Don't imagine orange groves or anything. Make your mind a blank. Just imagine that you are in perfect harmony with everything around you . .

ISIDORE

Wait, I have to erase the orange grove.

LEOPOLD

Forget about the orange grove.

ISIDORE

I can't forget the orange grove. It's planted in my mind. I have to uproot it. You put things in my mind and then it's I who have to get rid of them. At least leave me in peace for a moment, while I do the work.

LEOPOLD

I didn't put anything in your mind.

ISIDORE

You said, "Don't think of an orange grove." You did, didn't you?

LEOPOLD

Yes . .

24

ISIDORE

Well, the moment you said that, an orange grove popped into my head. Now give me time while I get rid of it. (*Isidore moves about the room as if he were picking up oranges and throwing them over a fence with his eyes closed. Leopold's impatience increases.*) First I'll throw this orange over the fence. Then, this little orange. Then this orange orange. Now this rotten orange. Now I pull this whole branch off the tree. Oh, oh, it's hard. Now I pull this other orange off the tree. Oh, oh, there are so many. There are thousands and thousands and I think millions and trillions. Oh, I'm tired. No, no, I must not rest. I can't take a moment's rest until I clear away all this mess of oranges. Thousands and thousands of acres, and then I have to clear the other side of the fence, and then the other, and then the other, and then dismantle the fence, and then the other fence, and then . . (*Leopold reaches for the pitcher of water and empties it on Isidore. They remain motionless for a moment. Isidore goes to his shrine and sits in his typical angry position. Leopold walks to the opposite end of the room and sits down.*) I'll never trust you again. (*The lights fade out. Isidore laughs out loud as the curtain falls.*)

SCENE 2

The curtain rises with Isidore and Leopold in the same position as at the end of the first scene.

ISIDORE

> Isidore I beg you.
> Have you no heart?
> You play games,
> And I'm so earnest.
> Isidore I beg you.
> Can't you see
> You're breaking my heart?
> 'Cause while I'm so earnest,
> You're still playing games.

Sung and composed by Isidore. Sixteen years old. (*card*) (*Leopold looks at Isidore*) Stop looking at me like that.

LEOPOLD

Like what?

ISIDORE

(*accompanying himself with the guitar*) Like a lover. Transfigured by the presence of the beloved. Looking as though you want to breathe the minute bubbles of air imprisoned in each of my pores. (*card*) Or like a drug addict who imagines specks of heroin concealed in those beloved dimples. (*card*)

LEOPOLD

And you think that's how I'm looking at you, you slob?

- ISIDORE

I'm offended. (*pause*) Come and make up with old Isidore.

LEOPOLD

Leave me alone.

ISIDORE

You'd die of boredom if I left you alone . . (*pause*) You'd have to come to me sooner or later. Come now. (*pause*) What if I don't take you later?

LEOPOLD

The better for me.

ISIDORE

I'll count up to ten.

LEOPOLD

Count up to ten.

ISIDORE

Don't be a stubborn brat.

LEOPOLD

Leave me alone.

ISIDORE

(*takes the Persian helmet and sets it on Leopold's head*) I'll let you wear it for a while. There's my baby. Isn't he cute. (*Leopold takes the helmet off*) See how contradictory you are? When I wouldn't lend it to you, you wanted it. Now that I'm willing to lend it to you, you don't want it.

LEOPOLD

Oh, go to hell. You twist everything.

ISIDORE

Now you're being rude.

LEOPOLD

Go back to your hole. (*Leopold picks up some cards and begins to sort them*)

ISIDORE

My hole. My hole? (*Isidore looks through his cards*) He means my shrine.

I think I will. (*Isidore goes to the shrine doing a dance step*) Peekaboo. (*Leopold stands in front of Isidore*)

LEOPOLD

Listen to me.

ISIDORE

Yes.

LEOPOLD

You're going to start behaving from now on. (*Isidore nods in consent*) OK. That's all. (*Leopold goes back to the cards. Isidore passes wind through his lips.*)

ISIDORE

So I'm going to start behaving from now on. Then what? . . Stop being silly. What is the matter with you, young man? You should be ashamed of yourself. What is life without humor here and there? A little bit of humor . . Look at him sorting out his little cards. He's a good boy.

LEOPOLD

I'm not sorting them. I just don't want to listen to you.

ISIDORE

You can't tear yourself away from them. Can you? . . You think I haven't seen you running to your cards the moment you think I'm not looking?

LEOPOLD

That's a lie. I've never . .

ISIDORE

I never lie. I have never lied in my life. (*card*) (*Isidore crosses himself, then covers his head as if to protect himself from lightning*) So what if I'm a liar. Do you think truth matters? Well, it doesn't. (*card*) Does that confound your infantile mind? It is order that matters, whether there's order or disorder. (*card*) A sloppy liar is despicable (*card*), as despicable as a sloppy truth teller. (*card*) Now, what do you deduce from that?

LEOPOLD

That you're rotten. (*Leopold flips a card to Isidore. Isidore sniffs himself.*)

ISIDORE

A systematic liar, a man with a goal, a man with a style is the best sort. (*card*) The most reliable. You'll never amount to anything until you learn that. No, you'll never amount to anything. You'll never make it in the army, the navy, politics, business, stardom. You're worthless. I'm almost tempted to give you the key.

27

LEOPOLD

Give it to me.

ISIDORE

Never mind that. Come here. I'm about to forgive you . . Come now. You really don't want me to forgive you?

LEOPOLD

Where is it, Isidore?

ISIDORE

Oh, here, in my heart.

LEOPOLD

Where is it?

ISIDORE

Oh, you're so insistent. I'll tell you what. (*Isidore takes the horns and the cape*) I'll answer all the questions you want if you do a little thing for me. Be a good bull and charge. Then I'll answer your question.

LEOPOLD

You'll tell me where the key is?

ISIDORE

Yes. Charge six times and I'll give you the key . . But you won't be satisfied with the key. On the contrary, it's when you have the key that you'll start asking questions. You'll start wondering about the mysteries of the universe. (*counting the banderillas*) One, two, three, four, five, six mysteries has the universe. As I stick each banderilla on your back I'll reveal the answer to a mystery. And then . . (*taking the sword*) the moment of truth. Right through the back of your neck . . Oh, beautiful transgressions. While I'm answering your last question you'll be expiring your last breath. As eternal verity is revealed to you, darkness will come upon your eyes . . Fair? Fair. Charge.

LEOPOLD

Are you kidding?

ISIDORE

I am not kidding. I am proposing the most poetic diversion ever enjoyed by man. You mean to say you're not willing to die for the truth? (*Isidore rubs his fingers to indicate "shame"*)

LEOPOLD

And when I'm crawling and bleeding to death begging you to answer my questions you'll say something like . . Ha, ha.

ISIDORE

You want to play or you don't want to play?

LEOPOLD

I'll play. But I'll only charge six times. Six passes. I only want one answer. No mysteries.

ISIDORE

All right. Ask your question.

LEOPOLD

Where is the key?

ISIDORE

Charge.

LEOPOLD

Answer first.

ISIDORE

The answer after you charge. (*Leopold begins to charge*) Wait. I lost the mood. I need preparation. (*Isidore kneels in front of the shrine and crosses himself. He makes a trumpet with his hand and toots a bullfighter's march. Isidore performs the passes as he calls out the passes' names.*) Toro and bull. Fearless, confident, and dominant, without altering the composure of his figure. Isidore lifts the spectators from their seats as he receives his enemy with "Veronica."

LEOPOLD

One. (*Isidore turns his back toward the audience*)

ISIDORE

Turning his back to the planks below the box occupied by the Isidore Fan Club to whom he has dedicated this bull. He performs a dangerous "Revolera." Marvelous both in its planning and development.

LEOPOLD

Two.

ISIDORE

"Faroles." And the embellishment.

LEOPOLD

Four.

ISIDORE

Three. A punishing pass. "Pase de castigo." All of Isidore's passes have identical depth and majestic sobriety.

LEOPOLD

Four.

ISIDORE

"Manoletina." Astounding elegance and smoothness. The music breaks out and competes with the deafening clamor of the multitude.

LEOPOLD

Five. (*Isidore bows, Leopold charges*)

ISIDORE

Then, with authentic domination, he performs the "Isidorina." (*Isidore circles the stage and bows*) Ovation. One ear. Turn. And cheers.

LEOPOLD

Six. Answer.

ISIDORE

Gore me.

LEOPOLD

Answer.

ISIDORE

Gore me. That's the answer. (*Leopold charges against Isidore, this time determined to get him. Isidore avoids him with a banderillero's turn while he thrusts a banderilla into Leopold's back.*) Saint Sebastian! (*Leopold falls to the floor. Isidore kneels beside him and holds him in his arms.*) Good bull. He attacked nobly and bravely. His killer made him take fifty-one passes and he would have continued charging, following docilely the course marked by deceit. He was cheered as he was hauled out, but less than he deserved. (*Isidore pulls out the banderilla from Leopold's back and caresses him tenderly. Leopold looks at Isidore imploringly. Isidore kisses Leopold.*) I have no alternative.

LEOPOLD

Don't tell me that, Isidore. I can't believe that.

ISIDORE

I have no alternative, Leopold.

LEOPOLD

No alternative? The alternative is simple.

ISIDORE

It isn't simple. I can't be good to you.

LEOPOLD

Just try.

ISIDORE

It's not within my power.

LEOPOLD

Have you no will then?

ISIDORE

No, I don't will it.

LEOPOLD

Who wills it?

ISIDORE
You, Leopold.

LEOPOLD
Me? It is not me, Isidore. You can't be right.

ISIDORE
It is you, Leopold.

LEOPOLD
I have never provoked you. I have never wished for anything but kindness from you. I have never tried but for your love.

ISIDORE
Yes, and maybe it is just that. Maybe you have been too patient, too good-natured. (*Leopold is astounded. There is a moment's pause. He then struggles with Isidore to break from his embrace.*)

LEOPOLD
You are rotten . . What are you? What are you that you must have rottenness around you? I am too patient? Too good-natured? I will not become rotten for you. I will not become rotten for you. (*Leopold holds Isidore by the neck and tries to strangle him*)

ISIDORE
(*gasping for air*) Son . . son . . let me tell you . . let me tell you . . a story . . There was once a man . . who . . (*Leopold covers his ears*) It's very important. You must listen. There was once a man whose only companion was a white rat. He loved this white rat dearly. And one day the rat disappeared. The rat couldn't have left the room, because there were no doors, or windows, or even cracks on the walls or floor. Then the man, thinking that the rat could have hidden in some nook or cranny unknown to him, took his axe and wrecked everything he owned . . The rat was nowhere in the room. He then turned to a picture of the rat which was hanging on the wall, and was about to wield his axe against it . . but he stopped himself . . He said, "This is the only thing I have left of my rat. If I destroy the picture, I will have nothing to remind me of him." And from that moment on, he began to speak to the picture of the rat and to caress it, and even feed it. Eventually, though, his loneliness brought him to such a state of melancholia that he no longer cared whether he was happy or not. He did not even care whether he lived or died. And as if he were summoning his own death, he picked up his axe and smashed the picture of the rat. There, trapped in the wires that supported the picture, was his beloved rat, who had died of starvation. The dead rat turned his head to face the man and said (*as if imitating a ghost*) "If you had not been

31

satisfied with my picture you could have had me. You chicken-hearted bastard," and then disintegrated into dust.

LEOPOLD

(*frightened*) A fairytale.

ISIDORE

There is a moral to it, Leopold. Try to understand it.

LEOPOLD

The dead don't speak.

ISIDORE

Yes, they do. You'll see, you'll see. Understand the story, Leopold. You must relinquish what you want or you will never have it.

LEOPOLD

I understand one thing. There is something that moves you. There is something that makes you tender and loving, only one thing: nastiness . . and meanness and abuse.

ISIDORE

Those are three things, Leopold.

LEOPOLD

They're all the same.

ISIDORE

It's our fate.

LEOPOLD

Not mine . . I love . .

ISIDORE

You don't love. Don't you see that all you do is whine? (*Leopold cries*) I had to tell you.

LEOPOLD

It's time you answer my question, Isidore.

ISIDORE

I answered it.

LEOPOLD

You told me to gore you.

ISIDORE

Yes, I did.

LEOPOLD

Is that the answer?

ISIDORE

That was my answer.

LEOPOLD

You stabbed me. I want my answer.

ISIDORE

There is a way, Leopold, but only one. You must find it yourself.

LEOPOLD

That's no answer. You wounded me.

ISIDORE

You tried to gore me. I had to defend myself.

LEOPOLD

You told me to gore you.

ISIDORE

That was part of the game.

LEOPOLD

Stinking bastard. Can you bear your own rottenness? You must atone for your wickedness sometime. You cannot go on and on without a purge. Do you ever pray? Do you beat your fist against your chest and ask for forgiveness? If not to redeem yourself, at least to be able to go on with your viciousness. You could not endure it without a purge . . Do you spend your nights covering your ears to keep away the sound of my moans? Do you cry then? . . Could it be that you do it out of stupidity, that you don't know the difference between right and wrong? Oh no. Let it be anything but that. Let it be malice. If you do it out of a decision to be harmful, I can convince you that it's best to be good. But if you don't know the difference between right and wrong, is there anything I can do? Maybe you must be vicious in spite of yourself. Maybe you have to do it . . to protect me from something worse? . . for my own good? (*Leopold throws himself on his knees with his head on Isidore's lap*) Give me a sign, a smile, a look. Tell me you love me. (*Isidore pouts innocently. He makes a circle with his arm and places his hand on Leopold's head. The lights fade.*)

SCENE 3

Isidore and Leopold are in the same position. Isidore stretches himself and yawns. He jerks his thighs slightly to make Leopold's head roll and fall to the floor. Isidore looks at Leopold who is waking up and smiles. Isidore stands up, stretches again, and does a dance step.

ISIDORE

Cheery-uppy, Leopold. (*The following scene is to have a nightmarish quality. Isidore and Leopold dance in a ritualistic manner. Isidore puts on one of the two beetle masks, the one which is wingless, and gives the other to Leopold. Leopold should behave like a sleepwalker.*) Beetles are versatile little animals. For great numbers, the end of autumn does not mean the end of their lives. There are more beetles by far than any other kind of insect. Over a quarter of a million beetle species have been described. Beetles are in constant conflict with man because there are few of the organic commodities that man has learned to use that do not also interest some beetle. Some spend their life in the thick flesh of century-plant leaves and when caught make an excellent salad, tasting something like shrimp salad. Other notable varieties are: The clavicornia, the segments of whose tarse are variable in number and whose antennae are equipped with a more or less (*Isidore does a bump and grind*) distinct club, the terminal segments being broader than the others. The Hydrophilidae (*Isidore places his arms in arabesque position*), Silphidae, Staphylinidae, Nitidulidae (*convulsing*), Histeridae, Coccinellidae, Ebdonnychidae (*holding his breasts*), Erotylidae, Languiridae, and Dermestidae . . The literature of beetles is enormous.

LEOPOLD

(*crawling on the floor*) When things are in disorder and I move, I feel like I'm crawling. As if with every movement I have to drag along with me the things that are in disorder. As if I had grown brooms on my sides that extend as far as the wall, to sweep the junk . . the dust. (*Leopold picks up some of the cards. Looks at Isidore and smiles sadly.*)

ISIDORE

They are for your own good. Ingrate. Don't you know? Come, do me a pretty beetle.

LEOPOLD

Dirt, my dear sir, comes to us from everywhere. And it comes out from within us. It comes out through each pore. Then we wash it away, we flush it away, we drown it, we bury it, we incinerate it, and then we perfume ourselves. We put odors in our toilets, medicinal odors, terrible odors, but all these odors seem sweet next to our own. What I want, sir, is to live with that loathsomeness near me, not to flush it away. To live with it for all those who throw perfume on it. To be so dirty for those who want to be so clean. To do them that favor. I wanted to drop it in the pot and leave it there for days, and live with it.

ISIDORE

Sometimes you touch the realm of romance.

LEOPOLD

In the latter part of the afternoon I feel cold. I feel the stuff in my bowels.

And I feel downcast. The open air is in my mind, but my eyes wander around this cave. I feel such pain for being here.

ISIDORE

The contrast between your poet's taste for languid amusement and my unconventional pageantry sends such fresh impetus throbbing through my veins . .

LEOPOLD

I see a light in you. The only light. I see it through a tunnel lower than myself. Attempting to go through it and hoping to be invited, I crawl.

ISIDORE

Crawl then. Crawl then. (*Leopold crawls*)

LEOPOLD

I liked to think I was an exception, of course, I pretended I was not one more snake. And to prove I was an exception, I tried to stand erect, and to stand erect I needed you to support me, and when you refused me I had to beg, and to beg I had to crawl, and snakes crawl, and I am a snake. When crawling tires me, I stand erect. It is to exhaustion and disillusion that I owe my dignity . . not to pride . . Oh . . I cannot make your eyes turn to me with love.

ISIDORE

Give me a pretty smile, pretty beetle. (*Leopold opens his mouth wide*)

LEOPOLD

To make dirt come out through the mouth you have to close your holes very tight, and let the dirt rot inside. Then it will come out through any opening.

ISIDORE

The prophet, the prophet. Come and hear the dirty prophet.

LEOPOLD

(*taking off his mask*) Oh, Isidore, you are my enemy and yet I love you.

ISIDORE

I am not your enemy.

LEOPOLD

Come here. Let me see you. (*Isidore moves near Leopold*) Take that mask off. (*Isidore takes the mask off*) You *are* my enemy.

ISIDORE

What makes you say that?

LEOPOLD

Your smell . .

ISIDORE

How do I smell?

35

LEOPOLD
You stink.

ISIDORE
Not true. What you smell is your own stink. You are putrid.

LEOPOLD
I'm going to kill you.

ISIDORE
Don't, you're trying to scare me. You're trying to scare me so I'll be good to you.

LEOPOLD
No . . I know nothing can make you change. No . . If I were to frighten you you'd behave for a while, but then you would get to like it, and you'd want more and more of it.

ISIDORE
And you wouldn't do it just to please your old friend?

LEOPOLD
No, I wouldn't. I have already played too many of your games. I have become as corrupt as you intended me to be. But . . no more.

ISIDORE
You can't stop now. It's too late.

LEOPOLD
I know. That's why I've decided to kill you.

ISIDORE
You have? (*Leopold goes to the shrine and gets the knife. Isidore hides behind a piece of furniture and begins to tremble.*)

LEOPOLD
Where are you?

ISIDORE
(*waving a white handkerchief*). Here.

LEOPOLD
Get up, Isidore.

ISIDORE
No. (*Leopold lifts the knife and holds it up for a moment, then lowers it slowly*)

LEOPOLD
If I killed you what would I be?

ISIDORE
A murderer . . that's what you'd be . . a murderer. A dirty ratty murderer.

36

LEOPOLD

There will be no one to judge me.

ISIDORE

Yourself . . you'll judge yourself. You'll die of guilt.

LEOPOLD

Guilt . . ? Is that what it is?

ISIDORE

Yes. And then you'll be all alone. You don't know what it is to be alone. It's horribly . . lonely.

LEOPOLD

I am afraid of my own death. I see myself dead.

ISIDORE

You're not going to do it then?

LEOPOLD

You're disappointed.

ISIDORE

Yes, I thought I was going to have some thrills and suspense, never knowing when you would strike . . having to sleep with one eye open. But as usual you are a party pooper . . You could never kill me, Leopold. Don't you see? You are just what I want you to be. You only know what I have taught you. And I haven't taught you how to kill.

LEOPOLD

You have offended me. If you died I still would be offended.

ISIDORE

I have offended you and you haven't challenged me to a duel? Challenge me to a duel immediately . . What kind of mouse are you . . I have offended you. I am offending you right now. You mouse. (*smack*) You mouse. (*smack*) You misbegotten mouse. You misbegotten lifeless mouse.

LEOPOLD

If I killed you the offense would not be undone. If you died, you would not be able to atone for it.

ISIDORE

Don't worry, there isn't a chance of that. I'll kill you and be done with you. (*Isidore puts the sword in Leopold's hand*)

LEOPOLD

If you killed me you would be convinced that you had the right to offend me.

ISIDORE

Beautiful, beautiful. Let's duel. You'll fight for your offended pride. I, for the right to offend you. Come on. Come on.

LEOPOLD

Please stop, Isidore.

ISIDORE

No, this is fun. It's fun. *En garde.*

LEOPOLD

(*poking different objects with his sword*) What are these things . . Leopold? Leopold? Are you Leopold? Are you . . They don't strike back. You are Leopold.

ISIDORE

Too much reflection. (*Isidore pokes Leopold with the sword. Leopold shrinks back.*)

LEOPOLD

Each time I hold back I die a little.

ISIDORE

That's why you stink, you're putrid with death. Cleanliness is close to godliness. (*card*) I still have a lot to teach you.

LEOPOLD

(*swaying*) I feel faint. If only I could find a spot to fix on and steady myself.

ISIDORE

(*swaying and lurching*) Look at me. Let me be the spot. Look, everything is moving. But I am steady as a rock.

LEOPOLD

Come here, Isidore. (*Isidore obeys*) Open your arms. (*Isidore obeys. Leopold lifts the sword slowly, points it to Isidore's heart, and pushes it into his body. Isidore falls to the floor.*)

ISIDORE

How could you do this? (*Leopold holds Isidore in his arms. He doesn't answer.*) Say you're sorry and my wound will heal.

LEOPOLD

I know.

ISIDORE

Say you're sorry.

LEOPOLD

If I do you'll curse me.

ISIDORE

I beg you, Leopold. I'm dying.

LEOPOLD

Die, Isidore . . I understand now . . You made it clear enough . .

(*Isidore dies*) It is done. All the thought and preparation did not help me do it. It is done. And I don't know what made me do it. The moment came. The only moment when it could be done. It possessed me and I let it take me.

The stage darkens. The door opens. The sound of harps is heard outside. There is a blue sky. Isidore appears among the clouds dressed as an angel. He carries stacks of cards. He beckons Leopold to follow him. Leopold picks up a few cards, then the sword, then a few more cards. Isidore shakes his head, and shows Leopold the cards he carries. Leopold walks through the door slowly, but with determination. He is ready for the next stage of their battle.

THE END

THE SUCCESSFUL LIFE OF
THREE: A Skit for Vaudeville

To Susan Sontag

Cast of Characters

THREE, a plump, middle-aged man
HE, a handsome young man
SHE, a sexy young lady
BODYGUARDS
POLICEMEN

NOTE. Three asterisks following a character's name indicate, for She, that She thinks with a stupid expression (the others watch her); for He, that He looks disdainful (the others watch him); and for Three, that Three looks with intense curiosity (the others watch him). Very deadpan.

THE SUCCESSFUL LIFE OF THREE

SCENE 1

The Doctor's Office. Three and He sit. He is combing his hair. Three takes a shoe off and drops it. At the sound of the shoe, He becomes motionless, his arms suspended in the air. Three looks at He, and freezes for a moment.

THREE

What are you doing?

HE

Waiting.

THREE

What for?

HE

For the other shoe to drop.

THREE

Ah, and I was wondering what you were doing. If I hadn't asked, we would have stayed like that forever. You waiting and me wondering . . That's the kind of person I am. I ask . . That's good, you know.

HE

Why?

THREE

* * *

HE

Why?

THREE

It starts action.

HE

What action did you start?

THREE

We're talking.

HE

That's nothing. We could as well be waiting for the shoe to drop. (*He suspends his arms in the air again. Three stares at He. They remain motionless for a while.*)

THREE

Sorry . . I'm going to do my sewing.

HE

First take the other shoe off. Get it over with.

THREE

(*taking his shoe off*) I wasn't going to take it off. (*Three takes needle and thread and sews a button on his shirt*) You see? If I do it now I don't have to do it later.

HE

What?

THREE

The sewing.

HE

And what are you going to do later?

THREE

* * * (*puts the needle and thread away*) Look, there are advantages to being optimistic.

HE

Sure.

THREE

What are they?

HE

You tell me.

THREE

Well, it makes one feel happier.

HE

You don't look happy to me.

THREE

Oh, no?

44

HE

No.

THREE

Well, things are not what they appear to the eye.

HE

They aren't?

THREE

Are they?

HE

Sometimes . . sometimes they are just what they appear to the eye . . Don't generalize.

THREE

Why?

HE

Because there are always exceptions. There's always one that isn't like the others.

THREE

If it's just one, it can be thrown in with the rest. It doesn't matter.

HE

It matters.

THREE

Perhaps you can exclude it in your mind. Without mentioning it.

HE

You have to mention it . . You're splitting hairs anyway.

THREE

I like splitting hairs.

HE

Well, do it when I'm not around.

THREE

I was just joking.

HE

(*correcting him*) Being facetious.

THREE

(*takes an apple from his pocket*) Want an apple?

HE

No.

THREE

An apple a day keeps the doctor away.

HE

I knew you were going to say that. (*She enters wearing a nurse's uniform*) Miss, you're a fine dish.

SHE

Thanks. (*exits and re-enters*)

HE

Miss, I would like to bounce on you.

SHE

Thank you. (*to Three*) Come in, please. (*Three and She exit; She re-enters*)

HE

Miss, I would like to bang you.

SHE

Your friend just did.

HE

Well, I'm next.

SHE

I only do it once a day.

HE

I get you all worked up and you do it with him instead?

SHE

* * *

HE

I'm handsome and sexy and I get you all worked up, and you go and do it with him? . . Answer now.

SHE

What?

HE

Is that natural?

SHE

I don't know. (*Three enters*)

HE

A moment ago I was thinking of marrying you.

SHE

You just saw me for the first time.

THREE

He figured he'd see you a few more times if he married you.

HE

Don't speak for me after you ruined everything . . Let me try again. Miss, would you go to the movies with me after work?

SHE

OK, I like the movies.

HE

Everybody likes the movies.

SHE

I never liked them until a few months ago.

HE

What made you like them then?

SHE

I saw a movie with the Lane sisters.

HE

You like them?

SHE

Yes, they're all right.

HE

What do they do?

SHE

Stupid things.

HE

Like what?

SHE

They cry and laugh.

HE

That doesn't sound so great.

SHE

I like it. It's all right if you like sisters.

THREE

I like movies about marriage, divorce, and remarriage.

SHE

I like sisters.

HE

I don't have any particular preference. I just like good movies . . with action and a lot of killing.

SHE

I couldn't go to the movies if I didn't have a preference.

THREE

Neither could I. (*takes She by the hand and exits; She re-enters*)

HE

Did you make it with him again?

SHE

Yes.

HE

How long are you going to keep this up?

SHE

I don't know. (*Three re-enters*)

HE

Listen, I was even thinking of marrying you.

SHE

You'd have to give me a ring for that. Two rings. An engagement ring and a wedding band.

THREE

I'll give the bride away.

HE

From the looks of it you're not leaving anything to give away.

THREE

And I'm not through yet.

HE

I didn't say you were.

THREE

You didn't say I was but you sure wish I were.

SHE

Me too.

HE

I never wish.

SHE

In my profession you have to wish.

THREE

For what?

SHE

* * *

HE

I don't have a profession.

SHE

How are you going to support me?

HE

I'll find a way.

THREE

He sure does have to support you. Doesn't he?

SHE

Yeah, my parents pay for the wedding and he supports me.

THREE

I'll pay for the wedding.

HE

He doesn't have any money. Get your parents to pay for the wedding.

SHE

Weddings are a pain in the neck.

THREE

Why do you want one then?

SHE

* * *

HE

Don't you see she doesn't know?

THREE

Yes, I see.

SHE

The Andrew sisters are all married.

HE

Do you like brothers too?

SHE

Not so much.

HE

Did you see the Corsican brothers?

SHE

That's not brothers. That's just Douglas Fairbanks playing twins. It's not the same.

HE

What brothers do you like?

SHE

I don't know any.

HE

How do you know you like them?

SHE

* * *

THREE

She didn't say she liked them.

HE

Didn't you say you liked them?

SHE

No, I said "Not so much" . . I don't think I'm going to marry you.

THREE

Why?

HE

I can ask my own questions, if you please. (*to She*) Why?

SHE

You're too picky.

HE

That's all right. Are we going to the movies or not?

SHE

Sure.

THREE

If you find a sister movie.

SHE

That's all right. I'll try another kind.

THREE

Let's go in for a quickie before you leave. (*Three and She exit; She re-enters wearing a hat*)

HE

Ready?

SHE

Yes.

HE

Hey, didn't you say you only do it once a day?

SHE

Yes.

HE

How come you did it with him three times already?

SHE

* * *

HE

You're not a liar, are you?

SHE

No.

HE

You better not be, because I can't stand liars. (*Three re-enters; He and She exit*)

THREE

Wait for me. (*exits*)

SCENE 2

The Movies. A few minutes later. The lights go down and flicker. He, Three, and She enter. They sit — Three in the middle, She and He at his sides.

HE

Hey, what do you mean by sitting next to her? Change with me. She's my date.

THREE

I can't feel her up from there.

HE

You don't have to feel her up. (*Three and He change seats*)

THREE

How about some popcorn?

SHE

I'll go.

THREE

Don't go. Let him go.

HE

You go.

THREE

I can't. (*He exits; Three moves next to She; He re-enters*)

HE

Move back to your seat.

THREE

I already moved once. I'm not moving twice. Let's have some popcorn. (*He offers popcorn to Three*) I'll hold it because I'm in the middle. (*Three tries to hold the bag, eat popcorn, and feel She up*) You hold the bag. I can't feel her up and eat at the same time if I hold the bag.

HE

(*takes the bag*) At least wait till the feature starts.

SCENE 3

The Porch. Ten years later. He dozes. She peels potatoes. Three sews.

SHE

I'm going to divorce him.

THREE

Give him another chance.

SHE

Him?

51

THREE
He's not bad.

SHE
Yes, he is.

THREE
There are worse.

SHE
No, there aren't.

THREE
Wouldn't it be worse if you were married to me?

SHE
What difference would it make?

THREE
It would make a difference.

SHE
No, it wouldn't.

THREE
Yes, it would.

SHE
What difference?

THREE

* * *

SHE
What difference?

THREE
I'll ask him. (*shakes He*) Hey, would it make any difference if she was married to me instead of you?

HE
Yeah.

THREE
What difference?

HE
Ask her. She ought to know.

THREE
She doesn't know.

HE
She never knows anything.

THREE
Actually, this time she knows. She said it wouldn't make any difference.

HE

She's probably right, because she usually doesn't know anything.

SHE

I'm going to divorce him whether I'm right or wrong.

THREE

Marry a worse one for a while . . then remarry him and you'll be happier.

HE

That would be like wearing tight shoes so it feels better when you take them off.

THREE

That's the idea. Do it.

SHE

You can't do that.

THREE

Why not?

SHE

I don't know.

THREE

(*to He*) Do you know why you can't wear tight shoes so it feels better when you take them off?

HE

No.

SHE

But isn't it true that you're not supposed to?

HE

Yeah.

SHE

I knew it.

THREE

Well, you'd be happier if you did it.

SHE

You're not supposed to.

HE

(*to Three*) Get off that chair. I want to put my feet up. (*Three moves to another chair*)

THREE

Rivalry.

SHE

What?

53

THREE
Rivalry.
SHE
* * *
THREE
Masculine rivalry.
SHE
* * *
THREE
Masculine rivalry. (*points to He and to himself*)
SHE
Whoever heard of such a thing.
THREE
What?
SHE
What you said.
THREE
Rivalry?
SHE
Yeah.
THREE
You haven't heard of it?
SHE
No.
THREE
I bet you he has. (*to He*) Have you heard of rivalry?
HE
Sure.
THREE
See?
SHE
I mean the other.
THREE
Masculine?
SHE
Both, both together.
THREE
(*to He*) Have you heard of masculine rivalry?
HE
Yeah.

SHE

So he has. (*Three looks She over*)

THREE

I don't desire you any more.

SHE

Thank God.

THREE

Don't thank God. Thank me.

SHE

Stop picking on me.

HE

Are you picking on her again?

THREE

I can't help it.

HE

Stop picking on her.

THREE

Masculine rivalry.

HE

What are you talking about? There's no comparison. I'm sexy and you're slimy.

SHE

That's the only thing I like about him.

HE

You like *that*?

SHE

It's all right . . But I'm tired of having children.

HE

That's not true. You told me you like children.

SHE

Not that many.

THREE

How many are there?

SHE

I don't know.

THREE

How do you know there are too many?

SHE

* * *

THREE

I'll go count them. (*exits*)

HE

Listen, you can't one day say you like babies and the next day say you don't.

SHE

Why not?

HE

You have to make up your mind.

SHE

* * *

HE

Well?

SHE

I can't stand the twins.

HE

Why not?

SHE

They look too much alike.

HE

Twins always do.

SHE

I didn't say they didn't.

HE

You didn't say they did either.

SHE

No, all I said was that I didn't like them.

HE

Why?

SHE

I don't see why they have to dress alike.

HE

Twins always do.

SHE

I didn't say they didn't.

HE

Bring the food out.

SHE

There's no food.

HE

How come?

SHE

You know how come.

HE

No, I don't.

SHE

You're supposed to provide for me, but you don't.

HE

Don't I get you all the potatoes?

SHE

I'm going, I can't stand peeling potatoes all the time. (*exits; Three enters*)

HE

She left.

THREE

Oh.

HE

That's all right. I never want what I don't have.

THREE

I missed it.

HE

What?

THREE

Her leaving. I've been waiting around to see her leave, and now she does it when I'm not looking. How did she go?

SCENE 4

The Porch. Three years later, He peels potatoes. Three sews.

THREE

I'm going into business. I can't stand this home life any longer.

HE

You wouldn't be any good at it.

THREE

I might as well try it.

HE

You would just lose all your money.

57

THREE
I don't have any money.

HE
How're you going to go into business?

THREE
I'll put a bid on some nylon rope, go south, convince the fishermen to use nylon instead of whatever they use, and take them for all they got.

HE
They probably use nylon.

THREE
Then I'll sell it to them cheap and still make a fortune.

HE
It wouldn't work.

THREE
No? . . Well, I can make a sandwich with peanut butter and Ritz crackers, dip it in chocolate, call it Tootsie Tootsie and sell it.

HE
You're better off with the nylon rope.

THREE
I thought so too. I'll go try it.

HE
OK.

THREE
Good-bye. Give my love to Ruth if you see her. Have you seen her?

HE
Yes, she's happily married.

THREE
Who to?

HE
I don't know.

THREE
Well, if you see her tell her I would still like a roll in the hay with her, even if she's getting old and decrepit.

HE
OK, I'll tell her.

THREE
Good-bye. You do think it will work.

HE
Sure.

THREE

Good-bye then. (*exits*)

HE

Just said that to get rid of him. (*Three re-enters wearing top hat and furs*)

THREE

It worked.

HE

Don't tell me it worked.

THREE

(*respectfully*) Oh, sorry.

HE

What do you mean it worked?

THREE

I put a bid on some nylon rope, went south, convinced the fishermen to use nylon instead of whatever they were using, and took them for all they had. D'you know rope is sold by the weight, not the measure?

HE

Don't get smart with me, Arthur. I'm very annoyed. I have all the brains and the looks and it's you who go south with your squeaky voice and sweaty hands and make all the money.

THREE

And I'm not finished yet. I'm going to make that peanut butter sandwich and make another mint.

HE

You're making me sick.

THREE

Don't get sick yet. I'm just starting. You think Ruth likes money?

HE

Sure.

THREE

Perhaps she'll come live with us for the money. It'll be good for the children.

HE

I'm the husband and the father. I'll make my own decisions.

THREE

Yeah, but I do all the screwing and make all the money.

HE

Don't rub it in.

THREE

Sorry.

HE

You may make all the money and all that but you have no manners.

THREE

Teach me manners. (*He puts on a top hat and furs; She enters*)

SHE

OK, I came back.

HE

Because of the money.

SHE

I like money.

HE

Everybody likes money. You say it as if it was something special.

SHE

It is special. I like money very much.

THREE

More than sisters?

SHE

* * *

HE

Never mind.

THREE

I have a present for you. (*gives She three men's hats*)

SHE

These are men's hats. What's the matter with you?

THREE

Nothing.

HE

He doesn't know his ass from his elbow.

THREE

I do. (*points to his buttocks and his elbow*) I only didn't know what kind of hat to buy.

SHE

Where's the money?

THREE

In the bank.

SHE

Oh, damnit. I came for the money and you put it away.

HE

You didn't come for that. You didn't come for that. You came for me
and for the children.

SHE

You said I came for the money.

HE

I was just accusing you.

SHE

And what was I supposed to say?

HE

"I didn't. I didn't. I came for you and the children." Defend yourself.

SHE

Well, I didn't.

HE

I don't have to stay here while you come back for his money. I'm sexy
and bright and you're a bunch of morons. I'm leaving. (*Three puts his
arms around She*) You don't have to jump on her the moment I turn
my back. (*Three lets go of She*)

SHE

I'm glad he caught you.

HE

You can do what you want. I'm leaving. Good-bye. (*exits*)

SHE

What are we going to do without him?

THREE

Wait for him.

SCENE 5

*The Store. Three years later. He is standing. Three enters and steals a
pipe.*

HE

Arthur!

THREE

What are you doing here?

HE

I'm a store detective.

THREE

How long have you been a store detective?

61

HE
Since I left the house.
THREE
Is the pay good?
HE
Not for the risk you take.
THREE
What risk?
HE
You might get hit or knifed.
THREE
Who would do that?
HE
The thief. You see, I grab him like this. I identify myself and I tell him to go with me to the office. Then he either becomes frightened and comes along quietly, or becomes violent and attacks me. (*Three punches He and runs*)

SCENE 6

The Porch. A few minutes later. She peels potatoes. Three enters smoking the pipe.

THREE
I just saw him. He's a detective.
SHE
I don't like detectives.
THREE
Why?
SHE
I can't understand them.
THREE
Why not?
SHE
They talk too fast.
THREE
He's a store detective. They don't talk fast.
SHE
A store detective is not a real detective.

THREE
Someone stole something though.

SHE
Did he figure out who did it?

THREE
I don't know. I hit him and ran.

SHE
You didn't run so fast. You're late for dinner . . Did you figure out who did it?

THREE
Yeah, I did it.

SHE
What did you do?

THREE
(*showing her the pipe*) Stole it. (*He enters*)

HE
Why did you hit me?

SHE
Is that a way to come in after you've been gone for three years? Can't you say hello?

HE
I don't feel like saying hello.

SHE
You could at least pretend.

HE
Why did you hit me?

THREE
Because I had to.

HE
Why?

THREE
Because I'm the thief and you're the detective.

HE
What did you steal?

THREE
Guess?

HE
I give up.

THREE
The pipe.

HE
Now I have to take you in.
THREE
You have to identify yourself.
HE
Don't be silly. You know me. Come on.
THREE
Good-bye, Ruth.
SHE
Good-bye.

SCENE 7

The Porch. Three days later. She and He are sitting.

SHE
How come you came back now?
HE
Because he's away . . Masculine rivalry.
SHE
That's what he always says.
HE
So what. It's true.
SHE
How come he was stealing?
HE
He didn't know he could take the money out of the bank.
SHE
Can he?
HE
Yeah. (*Three enters wearing a prisoner's uniform*)
THREE
I organized a revolt and got out.
HE
Can't you stay put in one place?
THREE
Can't I?
HE
No, you're always jumping from place to place.

64

THREE

I'll stay put now. Ruth, even if you're getting old and decrepit, I still want you. Jail makes a man want a woman.

HE

You disgust me. You spend three days in jail and you don't learn anything.

THREE

I did so. I organized the prisoners and now I'm the head of the mob. If you want I'll make you my bodyguard.

HE

You call that a body?

THREE

I know. I have to do some exercise. But in the meantime it's all right to call it a body.

HE

It is not all right with me. I'm leaving.

SHE

He's always leaving.

THREE

Like Shane . . Stay and have some fun. The guys are coming presently.

HE

What kind of idiot are you that says presently?

THREE

No idiot. I'm the Alec Guinness type gangster.

HE

Goddamnit. I'm getting fed up. You have no style, no looks, you act like an old housewife, and it's you who get to go to jail and become the head of the mob.

SHE

Let's eat.

HE

OK, but if you want me to be your bodyguard, you have to give me a good salary . . No. I don't care if you get slugged. Good-bye. (*exits*)

THREE

You be my bodyguard, Ruth.

SHE

OK, but I don't move from this chair.

THREE

You have to move. You have to keep an eye on me.

SHE

Skip it. Who wants to look at you all the time.

THREE

OK, don't be my bodyguard. I'll get the guys to look after me.

SCENE 8

The Porch. Six months later. Three and She sit. Three is armed to the teeth. Bodyguards surround him.

THREE

I have a sweet streak in me.

SHE

Where?

THREE

* * *

SHE

What did you say?

THREE

I have a sweet streak in me.

SHE

Me too.

THREE

I'm tired of the life of crime.

SHE

Why don't you stop stealing?

THREE

I like stealing.

SHE

I thought you said you were tired of crime.

THREE

Yes, but not of stealing.

SHE

You're not supposed to steal.

THREE

Says who?

SHE

* * *

THREE

You don't know anything. I'm going to steal from the rich and give to the poor.

SHE
I came back for the money and you're going to give it to the poor? I'm leaving.

THREE
Where are you going?

SHE
I'll go find a Joan Fontaine movie.

THREE
What good would that do you?

SHE
She's Olivia de Havilland's sister.

THREE
No, she's not.

SHE
Yes, she is.

THREE
They don't look alike.

SHE
The Lane sisters don't look alike either.

THREE
No, but they act like sisters.

SHE
* * * (*Three exits; She stands puzzled*)

SCENE 9

The Store. A few minutes later. He is standing. Three walks by surrounded by bodyguards.

HE
Come with me to the office. You penny-pinching son-of-a-bitch hoodlum. I finally caught you.

THREE
What for? I just came to get a Zorro costume. (*Three puts on a Zorro costume*)

HE
You look like an idiot, like you always did. Did you steal it?

THREE
I bought it.

HE

Show me the sales slip.

THREE

I lost it.

HE

You stole it. (*to the bodyguards*) Did he steal it?

BODYGUARDS

Yeah.

HE

Come with me.

THREE

Don't be silly. If I'm Zorro and the store is rich, I have to steal from it. Now I have to give something to the poor. Here's a penny.

HE

I'm turning you in anyway. I'll get fired if I don't catch someone soon. I haven't caught anyone since the last time I caught you. Get moving.

THREE

No, I won't. I have better things to do, like ride around the pampas with my mask on. Come with me and you can ride too.

HE

What kind of idiot do you think I am. You'll make me do all the riding and cut all the Z's and you'll get all the credit. You do your own dirty work.

THREE

No, I won't . . I'm getting too old to ride around like an idiot.

HE

You used to do your own dirty work.

THREE

Yeah. But now I'm rich and lazy. (*to a bodyguard*) Can you ride? (*the bodyguard shakes his head*) Can you ride? (*the second bodyguard shakes his head*) Can you ride? (*the third bodyguard shakes his head*) Get out of my way. I don't need you anymore. (*to He*) Can Ruth ride?

HE

No, she can't do anything.

THREE

That's all right. I'll go to some rodeo and get myself a double. (*exits*)

SCENE 10

The Porch. Three days later. He sits. Three enters panting.

THREE

Hide me.

HE

What from?

THREE

I'm being followed.

HE

What did you do?

THREE

I got tired of stealing from the rich and giving to the poor and started stealing from the rich and the poor. Hide me.

HE

I won't hide you, I don't care if they catch you.

THREE

Hide my *antifaz* then.

HE

What's that?

THREE

My mask. Do you know that Zorro means fox in Spanish?

HE

Never mind. I don't care if Zorro means fox. I can't hide your *antifaz*. I'll lose my job if I get caught with stolen goods.

THREE

I thought they were going to fire you.

HE

I caught a girl who didn't do anything and they let me stay.

THREE

That's not nice. Where's Ruth?

HE

She went to see Joan Fontaine and never came back.

THREE

Did she take any money with her?

HE

She doesn't need any money. She married the guy who owns the movie.

THREE

How're the children?

HE

They're all right. They're always playing doctor.

THREE

Are they sick?

HE

No, they just play doctor. (*the policemen enter and grab Three*)

THREE

Where're you taking me?

POLICEMEN

To the scaffold.

THREE

Oh! Merciful God. (*The policemen take Three away. Three re-enters.
He carries a bouquet.*)

HE

I thought they were going to hang you.

THREE

I got out of it. Here's Ruth. She must have broken up with that movie
man. (*She enters; Three gives her the flowers*)

SHE

How did you know that I was coming?

THREE

I didn't.

HE

How did you get out?

THREE

I told them you did it.

HE

I'll lose my job at the store.

THREE

Don't let that worry you. You won't need a job anymore. They're coming to get you any minute. (*to She*) What made you come back?

SHE

I'm old and tired and I've had too many men. I'm just going to sit here
and rest for the rest of my life.

THREE

Oh, no, you won't. You have to work for your keep. Scrub the floor.

HE

I'm going to the store. I can't stand seeing my wife scrubbing floors.

SHE

Don't go. I'm not going to scrub floors. You've become a mean old son of a bitch, Arthur.

THREE

I was always mean. I just didn't know it.

SHE

You're not supposed to be mean.

THREE

Why not?

SHE

* * *

HE

She's right. You're not supposed to be mean.

SHE

I knew it.

THREE

Well, perhaps I just have a mean streak in me.

SHE

Yeah, like the Grand Canyon.

HE

The Grand Canyon is not a streak.

SHE

What is it?

THREE

It's a ditch.

SHE

Same thing.

THREE

Well, here are the cops anyway. They're coming to get you.

HE

You're disgusting. You go around being a son of a bitch and then you pin it on me. What am I going to do now?

THREE

* * *

SHE

* * *

HE

You're a bunch of morons. (*the policemen enter and grab Three*)

THREE

Where are you taking me?

POLICEMEN

To the scaffold.

THREE

I just came from there. (*the policemen take Three away*)

SHE

Are you going to miss him?

HE

No, he's a son of a bitch . . are you?

SHE

What?

HE

Going to miss him?

SHE

* * * (*Three enters with a bouquet of flowers and gives them to She*)

HE

How come you always come back with flowers?

THREE

They have them there.

SHE

What for?

THREE

For the grave.

HE

Did you steal them?

THREE

No, they give them to you.

SHE

They go bad if they don't use them.

HE

How did you get away this time?

THREE

They caught the real Zorro.

SHE

I thought you were the real Zorro.

THREE

No, I'm too young.

HE

Bring in the food, Ruth.

SHE

What food?

THREE

I have some Tootsie Tootsies. (*They eat Tootsie Tootsies. A policeman enters. Three shoots him dead.*) I'm not armed to the teeth for nothing. (*They freeze for a moment. Then they sing the song to Ignorance.*)

SHE, HE, AND THREE

> Let me be wrong.
> But also not know it.
> Be wrong,
> Be wrong,
> And, oh, not to know it.
> Oh! Let me be wrong.

THREE

> One day while walking
> Down the street,
> I found a petunia
> And took it.
> I took it.
> Oh! Let me be wrong.

SHE, HE, AND THREE

> Let me be wrong.
> But also not know it.
> Be wrong,
> Be wrong,
> And, oh, not to know it.
> Oh! Let me be wrong.

SHE

> I went from here

HE

> To where?

SHE

> I don't know where.
> I called a parasol an umbrella.
> Yes, an umbrella.
> Oh, let me be wrong.
> I don't care.

SHE, HE, AND THREE

> Let me be wrong.
> But also not know it.

73

Be wrong,
Be wrong,
And, oh, not to know it.
Oh! Let me be wrong.

HE

I sprechen Sie Deutsch very well
I said to Herr Auber;
Herr Auber, I sprechen Sie
Deutsch very well, Herr Auber.
Oh! Let me be wrong.

SHE, HE, AND THREE

Let me be wrong.
But also not know it.
Be wrong,
Be wrong,
And, oh, not to know it.
Oh! Let me be wrong.
Oh! Let me be wrong.
Oh! Let me be wrong.
I want to be wrong!

They repeat the song as they walk the aisles selling Tootsie Tootsies.

THE END

NICK BORETZ

Shelter Area

Shelter Area by Nick Boretz was presented on November 19, 20, 21, 24, 25, 26, 27, 28, 29, 1964, at the Shevlin Hall Arena Theatre, University of Minnesota, Minneapolis. It was directed by David Miller.

Cast of Characters

FLESHER	Brian Hansen
GRAZZO	William Switky
KIT	Joseph Karioth
WOODY	Kenneth Frankel
EVA	Susan Abdallah

PLAYWRIGHT'S PREFACE

The play presented here is somewhat similar to the original idea. Through the infiltration course of production many changes occurred. This whole business is unimportant now. I changed my mind many times about what the play meant, but there was always something that kept bringing to mind a musty kind of dead temple or Greek antiquity. In this play's ending is woven the grotesque pathos which tragedy has become.

I am grateful that the production of *Shelter Area* came off under the guidance of the Office for Advanced Drama Research. The production combined with critical evaluations gave me new directions in which to pursue my craft. This in itself is enough to show that the O.A.D.R. is not just a good thing; it is a necessity.

There are no meanings to be discussed here as far as the play goes. The ensuing action, I hope, will reach a focal point far behind the eye.

NICK BORETZ

Beverly Hills, California
Summer 1965

THE PLAY

Cast of Characters

FLESHER   GRAZZO   KIT   WOODY   EVA

The Scene

The basement of the "Happyland Toy Company" in an eastern city. There are no windows as we are now below ground. Above, pipes run across the ceiling. To the right and left are huge shelves and wire bins of toys, which appear as columns. There are all kinds of toys here, from a five-cent silver-coated plastic whistle to an erector set and launching pad apparatus which can cover half a block. There are dolls, guns, whistles, boats, trains, etc. In the center of these racks is a long shipping table with a telephone, rolls of wrapping paper, tape machines for sealing, string, typing machine, decorative paper, paper cutter, stamp machine, scales. Mailing bags to left. An air chute for orders to come down. Down left is the men's room. We can see into it up to the door within the entrance door. From the entrance door to the door leading to the toilets is a little rest area with a couch and a place with lockers and coat hooks. Everything is dusty colored. Lighting is by overhead fluorescent. The floor is littered with papers. Off right is the elevator to the upstairs, and there is a back entrance with stairs, barely seen behind the racks, and with a sign over the door, DELIVERY ENTRANCE. Also another sign over the door, THIS PLACE IS DESIGNATED AS A SHELTER AREA. There is an intercom on a post to the rear. A wire box container is below the shipping table. There are shipping boxes which come in different sizes.

SHELTER AREA

ACT ONE
Scene 1

At rise, the stage is dark. Suddenly there is a burst of machine-gun fire from up left, high above the shipping room floor. The machine gun is a toy which throws out sparks and sounds like the real thing. Another burst of fire comes from a bin down right. This continues for about a minute, the bursts coming from different places as the men move around. They make noises: "Ya missed, ya bastard." "Take that, ya bum." *The bursts come together in a deafening roar and continue solid. Kit, the head of the basement, enters in the darkness and throws on the lights.*

KIT

Hey, hey! What is this? Flesher, Grazzo . .

GRAZZO

Greetin's an' salivations . .

KIT

Yeah . . well upstairs they're beginning to think there's a war going on down here.

FLESHER

Ha, ha, ha . . Just a small one. We was only testin' out th' new shipment of machine guns . . They check out.

KIT

I heard! Mark that shipment for Penny's OK. We'll haul it upstairs.

FLESHER

Sure. (*He starts putting machine guns in wrapping paper. Kit reaches under the table, pulls out a squirt gun, and gives Flesher a couple of shots in the back while Grazzo looks on. Flesher looks around. Grazzo laughs.*)

KIT

Lousy pipes in the building. Copper piping is the only thing to use . . (*hides squirt gun*)

FLESHER

Yeah. Hey, you hear th' joke about the . .

KIT AND GRAZZO

Yeah!

FLESHER

(*resigned*) Yeah . . I guess I told that one.

KIT

What do you say, erstwhile mailman? Through rain, sleet, snow, monsoon. Loses your mail for you every time. Aren't there any new jokes any more?

GRAZZO

Yak, yak. That's a joke? Listen, there's some guy outside who . .

KIT

Wait a minute. Here's a letter addressed to whomever it may concern. (*holds up a letter, rips it open*) Dear Happyland Toy Company. I . .

GRAZZO

Listen! Mister Mills . . no kiddin' . . there's this guy outside who started buggin' me about you while I was unloadin' th' truck. Then he started talkin' to some dame . . just started talkin' to some dame walkin' by . . blam!

KIT

What . . Who? You tell him we don't want any?

GRAZZO

Naw, he said he knew you . . looked a helluva lot like you as a matter of fact to be frank about it. Just like you . . only younger. (*Kit's expression turns serious*)

FLESHER

Hey, must be that same guy was down here earlier t'day when you was at lunch. Came in here, asked fer th' head of th' shipping department . . I told him th' men's room was right in there . .

GRAZZO

Haw, haw, haw.

KIT

(*after a pause, worried*) Oh . . He . . uh . . what did he look like? His name . . did he . . ?

FLESHER

Said he'd be back. Anything bad? If he comes down should I throw him out?

KIT

(*agitated*) You're sure . . you say he looked like me?

GRAZZO

Maybe it's th' hair . . same kinda hair . . (*pause*)

KIT

No . . no . . I'll take care of it . . I'll take care of it . . He . . didn't give a name?

FLESHER

Something like Wood . . or . .

KIT

(*has stooped at the shoulders slightly*) . . I can't believe it . . (*shakes his head*) OK, I'll take care of it . . excuse me . . (*moves into the men's room at the left, stands there, while Grazzo watches*)

GRAZZO

What's . .

FLESHER

You better get that other bag over to th' post office . .

GRAZZO

Yeah, OK. Hey, you gonna be at Eddie's Congo Room t'night? Yer pizza, y'know.

FLESHER

Ahhhh. (*waves him off. Grazzo backs off giving a glance into the men's room. During this section Kit has been standing in thought. He sits down, puts his head in his hands, then gets up again. He takes a locker door, which has been left open, slams it. Memories are coming into his head. His face is reflecting an old pain which his mind makes new, and his eyes stare off, squinting. Two voices are off right, those of Grazzo and Woody, who will appear momentarily.*)

WOODY

Is Kit Mills here?

GRAZZO

Yeah, right over there.

WOODY

Thanks, pal. (*The elevator begins to wind downward. Kit starts. Flesher looks off right. The elevator hits bottom. After a moment Woody appears. He is as tall as Kit, more muscular. He also wears glasses. On his forearm is a scar which is very prominent. He is dressed in an open shirt of Spanish origin. His hair is long and there is a boyishness about his face. Kit comes out of the men's room as Woody enters.)* Kit. *(There is a stoop to Kit's shoulders. He stands looking at Woody. After a pause, Woody continues.)* Hey, Kit . . *(another pause)*

KIT

(almost muffled) Hello, kid.

WOODY

(advancing forward slightly) My God . . The old place —

KIT

(after a pause) Uh . . Bud, will you go up and help Grazzo . . please . .

FLESHER

Sure . . You need me, yell! *(He goes off right. Elevator winds. The two men stand looking at each other, Kit with his head lowered.)*

WOODY

How've you . .

KIT

When did you get out, kid?

WOODY

(laughing nervously) Ha, ha, ha . . that's some greeting from your own brother . . When did you get out? Ha, ha, ha . . *(a pause, then continuing)* Yeah . . I got out a week ago. How did you know about . . that I was in jail?

KIT

Saw it one day in the paper . .

WOODY

You never came to see me . . *(pause)* Ah, well . . you know . . remember when we were kids . . that time you took out after Paul what's-his-name? You showed me how to take care of myself. Hell, I was seventeen . . you were nineteen then. This guy I . . I hit was just like Paul, Kit. Bullied the men at that warehouse where I had gotten a job. After I left home . . after the accident, I went to Europe . . then when I came back, I landed in the warehouse . . nine years ago. Guess I lost my head at this guy. I knew you woulda done the same thing. I hit him a little too hard, so . . Well, now I'm free . . clear. *(pause)* How've you been? You look great, Kit.

KIT

I've been all right. I got married while you were away . . girl you don't
know. Nice girl.

WOODY

That's good. Guess I still have that prison tan . . Ha, ha . .

KIT

What's up, kid?

WOODY

Oh . . well . . (*stops*) Look, I . . I wanted to come down here. Say
hello to you. God, it's been a long time.

KIT

Yes.

WOODY

A million years. Well, I've been looking for a job. Got myself fixed up
in a great attic downtown. There's a hole in the floor . . Ha, ha, ha.
(*pause*) But I haven't been able to find a thing to work at. I get to a place,
fill out the employment form and I get to the part that says "give refer-
ences . . where've you been working the last few years." That's a joke,
Kit. I look at it and I start laughing. (*stops*) I need a job, pal. (*pause*) Hey,
we're buddies, aren't we?

KIT

(*unable to look at him*) Kid . .

WOODY

(*quickly*) Now . . now wait . . a lot of time has passed since . . the
car accident and . .

KIT

(*interrupting*) Kid, I just don't know of anything around now. I don't
know.

WOODY

Ah. Well . . I . . I've had a lot of time to think about what I did . .
driving that car and Dorothea and Dad . . dying from the crash . .
and . .

KIT

I . . I'm sorry . . (*pause*)

WOODY

Yeah. Well, what the hell. You don't know of anything around, you don't
know. Ha, ha, ha . . (*pause*) Say, can you loan me a five? Haven't had
anything to eat since yesterday morning. They don't need a man here,
do they?

KIT

(*reaches in his jeans, pulls out a ten*) Here's a ten, kid.

WOODY

No, nope. Only need a five. I'll hook onto something.

KIT

Take it.

WOODY

Thanks . . then, they don't need anybody working here . . (*pause*) Look, Kit . . really. I'm a changed person from . . from when we were kids. I mean . . I want to get something steady. No more of that old . . you know . . bombing around. I went out to visit Dad's grave . . before coming here . . (*stops*) OK, OK . . Kit. Thanks. I know you'd tell me if you knew of anything. Well, what the hell. Maybe I'll see you . . another ten years. Soon as I make a little of the old money, I'll send you the ten back . .

KIT

Woody . .

WOODY

No, no . . God knows I haven't gotten to the stage of taking handouts. How would that be? A bum in the Mills family . . Ha, ha, ha . . (*stops*) So long, Kit. Take it easy. (*backs away*) Things'll work out. See you. (*turns*)

KIT

Kid, wait. (*pause*) I . . I can't promise anything but . . I mean . . I'll see what I can work out. (*pause*) Why don't you come back tomorrow . . nine in the morning . . take a bath, get yourself a good meal.

WOODY

(*stares at his brother; his voice is husky.*) Everything is OK . . then . . it's OK?

KIT

Sure, kid.

WOODY

(*with great honesty*) Kit, I swear to God, I'll —

KIT

Run along. See you in the morning.

WOODY

Sure . . sure. In the morning . . (*He backs out, turns, and goes. After a moment, the elevator winds upwards. Kit stands looking after Woody. The lights dim out after a moment to indicate a passing of time.*)

Scene 2

Two weeks later, late morning. Grazzo, Flesher, and Kit's voice coming from the intercom. He sounds nervous, expectant. The basement is unchanged.

KIT'S VOICE

(*over the intercom*) Bud, Woody there yet?

FLESHER

Naw, Mister Mills. He ain't come in yet. Called two hours ago . .

KIT'S VOICE

Yes, I know. He left to pick her up from his probation officer, but he hasn't come in yet?

FLESHER

Naw. (*pause*)

KIT'S VOICE

Two hours . .

FLESHER

You call th' station? You're sure yer wife got on th' . .

KIT'S VOICE

(*interrupting*) Yes, yes. (*pause*) Well . . if you hear anything let me know. I'll be down in a while. Put down I have a lunch appointment at one . . what the hell time is it now?

FLESHER

Eleven-thirty A.M.

KIT'S VOICE

Remember, if you hear anything . .

FLESHER

Right. (*There is a click from Kit's end. Flesher releases a switch, turns to Grazzo who is throwing mail in a bag.*) Ho! ho! . . Jesus how d'ya like that?

GRAZZO

Wha'?

FLESHER

He oughta get ridda that dame. You know what I'd do if I caught my wife actin' like that? I'd break her face f'her.

GRAZZO

Yeah . . She looks like one o' them babes outta nudie movies. She looks undressed with clothes on. (*flips his right hand up and down*) Sheeeee!

FLESHER

You! Ha, ha, ha . . Keep that up, you'll end up like Harris.

87

GRAZZO

You think Mills really got ridda him because . . I mean that's the reason Harris's over in Brooklyn now? Hah?

FLESHER

Sure! You remember how Harris talked to her down here. She gave him
that come-on. You saw her.

GRAZZO

Yeah. Then Kit had him fired.

FLESHER

Wouldn't you if you found some guy diddlin' yer wife? You nuts? You
know what I think? Guy can't control his own wife . . there's somethin'
wrong with a guy like that . .

GRAZZO

You think she's takin' out after Woody? Naw . . it's his own brother . .
She wouldn't pull that.

FLESHER

Grazzo, you gotta stop readin' comic books. She ain't Minnie Mouse,
y'know. Christ! You oughta get married. Looka me. Married twenty
years.

GRAZZO

You gotta good relationship. I gotta say that. Good relationship is important.

FLESHER

I say to her. Shuddup an' sit down! Simple. Shuddup an' sit down! Ya
gotta add that sit down part of it.

GRAZZO

Aha. Then what?

FLESHER

Then . . what. Whataya mean what? (*pause*) Ah . . well, then maybe
I take her out to a show or something y'know . . it's a philosophical
thing . . two people!

GRAZZO

Well, I almost got married once. She was ugly as hell.

FLESHER

That's good! Good! She won't run around . . nobody else'll want her.

GRAZZO

She was so ugly I din't want her. Help me with this bag, will ya? (*throws
mail to bag*) An' you need money to go out with 'em, y'know . . Now if
I was gettin' yer job when you step up to Kit's job . . You gonna really
get it?

FLESHER

Accordin' t'Woody. I got it knocked. Din't he say it about fifty times?
Sure! That's why Mister Mills' been havin' lunches with th' big guns
upstairs . .

GRAZZO

Head of basement operations at the Crappyland Toy Company . . Somethin' t'tell yer granchildren as a matter of fact. How can you be head
of the basement if you don't change yer socks?

FLESHER

Get outta here! Some people sweat a lot, y'know. Wise ass! I got seniority
here . . been working this hole fer ten years! I'll tell you a secret. I
don't get this upgrade . . I'll goddamn be ready to pull somethin' here.
Goddamn ready. I'll fix those bums up there . . They think we're a
buncha toys ourselves down here . . pull strings . . we jump up an'
down. Not me, Charlie. I'm fed up to th' teeth tied down here in the hell
hole. You get th' picture?

GRAZZO

You fed up, eh? I was fed up once. Boy was she ugly.

FLESHER

Tell me somethin'. You hungry?

GRAZZO

Me? Why?

FLESHER

Because I'm about to give you a knuckle sandwich is why! Get outta here.
Listen, when you get to th' post office you tell Hank Groshen stop throwin'
our stuff around . . I got too many breakage reports . .

GRAZZO

So what's new? I told 'em maybe a thousand times.

FLESHER

Tell 'em again. Get back here four sharp. You tell 'em again or I'll go
down there personally . . lousy bastards.

GRAZZO

Yeah, yeah . . (*hoists bag higher on his shoulder*) You gonna be at Eddie's tonight? My pizza.

FLESHER

Eight or around. Gotta get cleaned up here. Looka these orders.

GRAZZO

Y'know, I don't think I'd mind if you did blow up this place or somethin'
as a matter of fact. Blam! Toys all over New York. (*pause*) Hell. (*He
starts off right, but before he can move two feet Woody enters. He comes*

*down the steps to the back slowly. Woody has on a shirt which is slightly
ripped; his tie is flowing.*) Hey, look what somebody dropped out of th'
elevator shaft. Bugles blare, people cheer. Th' lover is here.

WOODY

(*preoccupied with something*) Yeah . . please no pictures . . (*pause;
he leans against a rack*)

FLESHER

Yer brother's been blowin' his brains out about you. Where the hell you
been for two hours? (*Woody takes his shirt off, looks at the tear, goes into
the men's room*)

WOODY

What? Oh . .

FLESHER

He's worried about his wife. Ha, ha ha, ha . .

WOODY

She's down the street at Folder's store looking at some stuff . .

FLESHER

You better let him know, he's . .

WOODY

She'll be over. She'll be here. (*pause*)

FLESHER

What took you so long?

WOODY

Oh . . say, what's on the agenda?

FLESHER

Energetic, ain't he. What happened? She made a pass at ya? You wres-
tling?

WOODY

What? What the hell's that supposed to mean?

FLESHER

Take it easy. You come in . . shirt ripped open . .

WOODY

Let's forget it, OK? What about that shipment I just saw on the dock?

FLESHER

It'll hold.

WOODY

Well, you call it then.

FLESHER

Take it easy. You've been here two weeks. You gotta slow down sometime. Never saw a worker like him, Grazzo . . Comes in here every

morning at seven-thirty and you can't turn him off. Siddown, take a break, have a cup of Sanka . .

WOODY

OK. (*flips a cigarillo into his mouth*)

GRAZZO

You still smokin' that rope?

WOODY

Mild tobacco, Grazzo. Say, Bud. Guess who I just happened to see on the street as I was walking in here? Remember that girl I met at the ballroom two nights ago? That redhead? Saw her on the street just as I was coming in here.

FLESHER

Ha, ha, ha . .

WOODY

(*getting involved*) She was carrying her laundry . . a bundle of priceless possessions, no doubt. She asked me to help her with her bundles. How about that, Grazzo?

FLESHER

Aah, don't listen to him. It's gonna turn out just like what happened down here last week . . Joker here. Stories . . Stories . .

WOODY

Bud, your cynicism amazes even me.

FLESHER

Awright. What th' hell ever happened to all th' nice secretaries you was gonna get down here to apply for th' secret undercover work. Ha, ha, ha . . One frowzy lookin' dame about a hunnerd years old falls in here, an' it takes joker here two hours to get her off his neck. To convince her it was a joke. Real bedside manner you got.

GRAZZO

Yeah. You was gonna get a thousand phone numbers.

FLESHER

She wanted his phone number. When Kit heard about that little joke, he got pretty mad, y'know. I'll let you in on a little secret. He almost kicked you outta here. Little old pink slip transfer. (*pause*)

WOODY

(*nervous*) Ha, ha, ha . . OK, OK . .

FLESHER

You laugh . .

WOODY

Come on . . (*slightly nervous*)

FLESHER
He said it.

WOODY
(*uncertainly*) Aaaah, you expect me to believe that? He didn't say anything to me. How do we get along with each other? We get along great . .

GRAZZO
What about th' bundles?

WOODY
Hell, Kit and I are like that. (*crosses his fingers*) Come on . . Ha, ha, ha. Right, Grazzo?

GRAZZO
Sure. Right. So what about th' . .

WOODY
(*slapping Grazzo on the back*) Oh, she requested that I come up to her place.

FLESHER
Why didn't ya go up there then?

WOODY
I have a girl, don't I? You know . . Ann . .

FLESHER
You mean that nut what keeps callin' you here?

WOODY
Bud, you have such a capacity for description . . "That nut what keeps callin' . . "

FLESHER
Why, yer real romantic, Woody. Yer real something.

WOODY
Few jokes . . get them laughing and then zero in.

FLESHER
Some time you'll kid around too much. Yer not the only one what can pull jokes. (*pause; to Grazzo*) With his stories about Spain and travelin'. He tells that babe in th' ballroom about his adventures. Then he says "and I also was in jail for manslaughter." Braggin' right in her nose. Don't tell me she even gave you a look outside here today . . if he even met her again. Hell, she screamed right in th' middle of th' dance floor that night and ran into th' can . .

GRAZZO
Ho, ho, ho, hey. I woulda like to see that.

FLESHER
Talk. Talk. All talk.

WOODY

Women like a few jokes . .

FLESHER

Aw, them whores like jokes. Like Harris. Remember, Grazzo? He was a joker too. He made it big with whores . .

GRAZZO

Yeah, ha, ha . .

WOODY

All I wanted was for her to join us over at Kit's place . . have a little party. He was a little down, probably because his wife's been away.

FLESHER

Sure. But now she's here . . ha, ha ha . .

GRAZZO

If she gets outta Folder's store. (*voices upstairs*)

KIT'S VOICE

Didn't know you were here. How d'you like that. Ha, ha, ha.

EVA'S VOICE

Yeah!

KIT'S VOICE

Where'd you get all the packages? What's? . .

EVA'S VOICE

Oh . .

KIT'S VOICE

Just a minute . . pigeon . .

WOODY

C'mon, Grazzo . . I'll help you with those bags.

GRAZZO

Hold it. That outgoing?

WOODY

Yeah . . come on . .

GRAZZO

Work, work. I want to see her.

WOODY

Come on. (*throws mailbag at Grazzo*)

EVA'S VOICE

What are you doing? I got some clothes.

KIT

(*arrives in the basement*) Bud, look, will you take care of that shipment up on the dock?

EVA

(*in the basement*) Well, how in the world can you tell me something like that? How could they do it again? I tell you I am completely fed up! You could have told me over the damn phone. My God!

FLESHER

I'll get on it. How are ya, Missus Mills?

EVA

How nice of you to ask.

FLESHER

'Scuse me. (*goes out the back.*)

EVA

(*to no one*) I'm great. Just great.

KIT

Hey, honey . .

EVA

You could have called me three days ago in California . . told me that they canceled your transfer again.

KIT

Why should I do that?

EVA

Because I wouldn't have had to come back to this . . this place . . This . . You know how I hate it here . .

KIT

What? You mean you would've stayed out there? What do you mean?

EVA

(*covering*) Oh . . You would've had to come after me then.

KIT

Oh . . Ha, ha, ha . . Well listen, pigeon . . just two weeks. Two weeks . . that's all. Then we're off.

EVA

And then at the end of the next two weeks . . again . .

KIT

No, I promise. Promise. Just . . take it easy. There's nothing I can do about it now . . so . . Let's just fall with it. (*kisses her*) . . God, I'm glad you're back. I nearly went crazy at that apartment alone. Everywhere I'd find something. Your shoe . . I know you're upset, but . .

EVA

Why weren't you at the station? Some guy tried to pick me up . . Where were you?

KIT

Business all morning. Woody got you, didn't he? Who tried to pick you up? Who was he?

EVA

Just my type. Well . . at least Woody got rid of him. They had a scuffle . . Ripped Woody's shirt. Ripped the collar.

KIT

Ha, ha, ha . . That's Woody . . How come you were so long?

EVA

First he drove me to the apartment. Found dirty dishes in the sink.

KIT

Must've forgot that. Really had to rush this morning.

EVA

Two weeks . . What a drag. I just . . this place is so . .

KIT

Hey, we'll do things together . . I'll take you out like I used to. You see the present at the apartment? Got you a five-pound box of candy . . you know . . those chocolates you go crazy over.

EVA

No.

KIT

Right on the Dux chair, honey.

EVA

I probably sat on them. How do you like my hair. I cut it again.

KIT

Looks great. You get more beautiful every time I turn around.

EVA

(*fluffing her hair*) No. It's terrible!

KIT

Ha, ha, ha . . You hate it long, then you cut it and even then you're not satisfied. Ha, ha, ha . .

EVA

So tired I could sleep for a week.

KIT

Bad trip? (*holds her, fondles her hair, and kisses her neck*)

EVA

No.

KIT

How are Mom and Dad?

EVA

You ought to know. You wrote them three letters while I was away . . one to me.

KIT

(*pause*) Gained some weight, didn't you?

EVA

Yeah. I can hardly get into these pants.

KIT

Yes, I got the picture. Maybe you shouldn't wear those around here.

EVA

Don't you like them?

KIT

Sure, but . . You know how these guys are around here. Guys in the basement are all sex maniacs. They sit around and read nudie magazines all day. They're crazy.

EVA

They are? That's exciting.

KIT

Rip the pants right off you.

EVA

Well, it shows they're alive, anyway. Some kid peed all over my suitcase. Two or three times. Everything stinks. So I had to buy these clothes . .

KIT

You should have let me buy you clothes.

EVA

Well . . (*silence*)

KIT

Look, why don't you call a cab, and I'll meet you at home later.

EVA

OK . .

KIT

That's my good girl, huh? You're tired, sleepy . . pants too tight. Ha, ha, ha . . Just two little weeks and we'll be flying right out of here. Promise. How I missed you. (*holding her close*)

INTERCOM

Mills? Hello . .

KIT

Yes . . yes, sir . .

INTERCOM

Coming up? We have a few things to run over . .

KIT

Be right up . . (*intercom clicks off; to Eva*) Gotta run, pigeon. (*holds her*) Can't wait till I get home. Maybe I'll take off early . .

EVA

Why?

KIT

Why? Ha, ha, ha, ha . . Here's some money. Get yourself a cab, will you. Get a fifth of Scotch. Tonight we'll celebrate!

EVA

OK.

KIT

(*kisses her*) Better call a cab. They're tough to get at this hour. (*He goes out, up the stairs. She goes to the telephone.*)

WOODY'S VOICE

Kit, I . . I'd like to talk to you . . alone . .

KIT

Yeah, a couple minutes . .

EVA

Give me the number of a taxi company . . No, no. Any taxi company, I don't care . . (*Woody appears in the basement*) Thank you. (*without turning, Eva says to him*) What's the address here, Woody?

WOODY

Fifteen hundred Second Avenue.

EVA

Please send a cab to fifteen hundred Second Avenue. Yes, that's right. Thank you. (*hangs up, turns to Woody*) You've been very helpful today.

WOODY

(*still watching her*) Thanks.

EVA

You're welcome. (*pause*) Tell me something. Woody, are you a sex maniac?

WOODY

What? Ha, ha, ha . . a sex maniac?

EVA

WELL?

WOODY

Oh . . yeah . . Sure. Sure I am. Ha, ha, ha . . that's me. At your service . .

EVA

I was getting worried down here . . Kit says this place is filled with sex

97

maniacs and . . that could be dangerous, but . . you'd protect me . . like you did at the station.

WOODY

Protect you? Sure. Look, these guys . .

EVA

Let's be friends. OK? (*puts out her hand*)

WOODY

(*nods*) Sure. (*shakes her hand, slightly confused*)

KIT'S VOICE

What about Perine's down the block?

OTHER VOICE

No, the weather's pretty damn warm.

KIT'S VOICE

Sure, leave your coat . . I'll be right up.

OTHER VOICES

Harry phoned for reservations? Reservation for lunch? Sure there's clean tables . . gotta have a reservation . . ha, ha, ha. (*Eva starts away*)

EVA

(*to Woody*) See you. I can mend your shirt for you.

WOODY

No, that's OK. I'll take it to the laundry. (*she smiles at him, starts out as Kit is coming down*)

KIT

You still here, pigeon? See you later, eh?

EVA

Lovely . . (*walks out*)

KIT

(*over to Woody*) Everything OK here? I'll be out at Perine's for lunch.

WOODY

Kit?

KIT

Why don't you take a lunch break. I'll send Bud down here . .

WOODY

No, I'm off at one-thirty. (*Kit puts on a shirt from a locker, opens another locker*)

KIT

What's this? This your stuff?

WOODY

Oh . . Not too much room at my place. I had to leave some things here.

KIT

Ha, ha, ha . . (*pause*) Well, how do you like her? (*pause*) What do you think of Eva, huh?

WOODY

It's . . it's remarkable, Kit.

KIT

Remarkable?

WOODY

Yes.

KIT

How so, kid?

WOODY

She, well, it's just that she looks quite a bit like . . well, like Dorothea . .

KIT

(*turns to him*) She looks like . . like who? Dorothea?!

WOODY

Yeah . .

KIT

No . . Like Dorothea? No, kid. I don't think you remember her very well if you think Eva . . No . . ha, ha, ha . .

WOODY

(*hurt*) I . . Look, I went out there today before going down to the station . .

KIT

What are you talking about?

WOODY

I was out at the cemetery. You were out there . .

KIT

Oh, yesterday. I put some flowers out there for Dad . . that flower place is starting to slack off on the contract . .

WOODY

Yeah . . I guess the ones on Dorothea's place blew away or something . . I put some there. (*pause*) When I got to the station, and I saw Eva . . I . . I mean . .

KIT

Well, you were probably thinking about where you had been . . visiting Dad. You probably had it on your mind and . .

WOODY

You really don't see the resemblance . .

KIT

(*changing the subject, slams a locker door*) Nope. Look, kid . . I want to thank you for going down there today to pick her up. That was very helpful. They had me running around like a chicken with its head cut off all morning. You stop and get those back orders for the automatic grasshoppers from Bernie's?

WOODY

Yes.

KIT

OK . . Where are they?

WOODY

(*pulling yellow slips from his pocket, puts them on the central table*) Two.

KIT

Get some lunch and then take care of that stuff. I should be back at two . . two-thirty.

WOODY

I'll take care of it right away.

KIT

Don't kill yourself, kid. You've really been working your tail off the past two weeks since you came to work here.

WOODY

Oh . . have to get back in shape. (*pause*)

KIT

You know . . you really have changed, Woody. It's amazing. I suppose it's a process of growing . . traveling like you've done. It's good.

WOODY

It's a forgetting process.

KIT

I . . I suppose so. You've kicked off a lot of your old habits . . fooling around . . joking . . your recklessness . .

WOODY

Well . . look, Kit . . the funny thing is that every time I'd do . . something like that . . you know . . joke around . . I'd get a picture in my mind . . of you.

KIT

Of me? How could that be?

WOODY

Yes. (*moves away*) I'd get this picture of you . . you know when we were kids around this neighborhood, how you led that gang around here. The

Syndicate . . playing jokes . . just living the way you wanted . . no restrictions . . nothing over your head . .

KIT

Ha, ha, ha, ha, ha . .

WOODY

Nobody could grab anything from you . . you used to have me tag along after you, and you knocked over anybody who pushed me around.

KIT

You didn't do too damn badly yourself sometimes you know.

WOODY

Sure, but you taught me everything I know. Dad was never around. Guess I kind of picked up that old recklessness . . (*pause*)

KIT

(*accusingly*) From me . .

WOODY

No, I'm just saying . .

KIT

You're just saying that every time you . . you did some careless . . reckless thing . . it was me there . . that's what you're . .

WOODY

Not at all. It was me. I was the one doing . . I don't blame . . I don't blame you for . .

KIT

I don't follow your line of reasoning. I think you've got to get it through your head that you build your own life, kid. You don't throw the blame for . . for the way you are on somebody else's head!

WOODY

(*annoyed*) Look, all I'm saying is that . . that maybe I remembered the wrong things, and now I . .

KIT

You've just always remembered what you've wanted to. Not the . . the important things . . My God, you have some kind of free will. Nobody becomes a Frankenstein monster in this world . . they . .

WOODY

Yes . . OK . .

KIT

(*with guilt*) You . . you have the ability to choose . .

WOODY

I understand that . . I have, Kit. I have here . .

KIT

Well, you always have . . but now you've . . you've grown in the past twelve years . . you've traveled in Europe, had a misfortune or two. In some ways I envy you. Hell, after I finished college, I settled here into Dad's old job.

WOODY

Yes, I knew this place was a bum joint when Dad worked here. They kept him around at all hours. No wonder he went down to Atlantic Beach on the weekends looking for girls.

KIT

Looking for girls . . Ha, ha, ha . . You're really funny . .

WOODY

Sure. You remember he went down with that straw hat on . . and white pants. He used to sit on the beach fully dressed. He hated the sun.

KIT

He'd come home with a tan.

WOODY

Yeah, the tip of his nose.

KIT

Ha, ha, ha . .

WOODY

That's where he met Dorothea . . in that bar. That beach bar.

KIT

Oh, he never met her in a bar. That was just a joke he used to pull on her. I knew she never met him in a bar . . not Dorothea.

WOODY

Sure. I saw her in there once. She knew everyone in the place.

KIT

(*pause*) She was . . she had a sense of adventure . . She couldn't be . . be tied down. Why, it is a crime to keep a girl like that in the house . .

WOODY

What?

KIT

You couldn't tie her down, you know? (*sees her in his mind*)

WOODY

No, I guess not. (*watching his brother*) She was quite a woman.

KIT

(*pause*) Uh . . Yes, she was quite a woman . . Oh, I got a job down here . . head of the basement at the Happyland Toy Co. . . They've promised me a transfer to the west coast, but so far . . problems . .

Eva hates it here in New York. She's just a hometown girl. She's been putting the spurs on me to transfer, but the company keeps stalling around.

KIT

WOODY

Pulling strings . . keep the employees jumping . .

KIT

Well, Eva and I will be out of here in a couple of weeks. Knock on wood. As long as everything moves along smoothly down here, which reminds me . . I was going to hit you over the head for bringing those women down here . . you know . . to apply for secretary jobs . . I realize you can still slip back to your old jokes, but it doesn't sit well upstairs . . you know. I don't want to . . harp on . .

WOODY

They . . they heard about that? How did you . .

KIT

Ha, ha, ha . . have to keep things on an even keel here. That way you'll keep your job, kid.

WOODY

Secret police . .

KIT

Hey, now . . I order you to get some lunch. Maybe, I can fix it. You can come with all of us . . Joe, Harry . .

WOODY

No . . no . . I . . I . . uh . . don't have a shirt. I tore it lifting some stuff . . some of those boxes. (*pause*)

KIT

Lifting some stuff — you mean that shirt you had on this morning? (*suspicious*)

WOODY

Uh . . yeah. That's right. I was . .

KIT

I was going to give you one of mine. Eva told me you got in a little . . a little hassle with somebody at the train and he tore your shirt.

WOODY

She . . she told you about that?

KIT

What do you mean? Why did you tell me you tore it lifting some . .

WOODY

(*interrupting*) Oh . . it was nothing . . forget it . .

103

KIT

Forget it! What happened out there, kid?

WOODY

She told you about it, didn't she?

KIT

Not the whole thing. Somebody accost her?

WOODY

No . . no . . It was nothing . . She was sitting in the lounge when I got there. He had his arm around her shoulder . . I didn't know who Eva was . . I mean . . what she looked like . . so I went to the information counter . . They had her paged. I saw Eva come to the counter . . This guy was following her . . I told the guy to beat it . .

KIT

Yes?

WOODY

Well, I told him to beat it . . so he put on this big act like Eva invited him to have a drink . . and what did she have to say about it? I . . I told her who I was . . and she said the guy had tried to pick her up . . so I asked him again if he'd beat it. He called her some names . . and I guess I hit him a couple of times . . he ripped my collar down . .

KIT

He said she'd invited him for a drink?

WOODY

That guy was . . he was a wise guy. (*pause*)

KIT

(*slightly nervous*) Sure . . sure he was. Should have called a cop . .

WOODY

Well . . I didn't think he'd get so . . so upset . . so . .

KIT

Yes . . yes . . (*as if in thought*) OK . . You did right then . . You did right . . (*silence*)

WOODY

Well . . I'll get some lunch later. Thanks for the invitation.

KIT

Oh . . don't . . uh . . say anything about this business at the station . . you know . . keep it under your hat . . You understand . . I'd . .

WOODY

I understand.

KIT

Fine. See you about two-thirty . . three . .

ACT TWO
Scene 1

A week later, night, the basement. Darkness, but for a red light which glows above the delivery entrance. At rise, there is a light on the stairs. Laughter. Kit, Woody, and Eva. Kit comes to the bottom of the stairs first, snaps on the lights.

WOODY

Here we are. Here we are.

EVA

(*carrying a small transistor radio*) Here we are.

WOODY

(*laughing*) The pit!

EVA

The pit. Ha, ha, ha . .

KIT

Woody, will you turn off that radio. Now listen, you two . .

EVA

(*pointing at Woody*) Now listen you two. Ha, ha, ha. (*Woody laughs; Eva waves a glass around*)

KIT

(*to Eva*) Where did you get that glass? Did you take that?

EVA

(*reading on edge of glass*) Joe's place. Twenty-seven-inch TV — call Tr. 65000.

WOODY

(*takes glass*) Let's see that. (*reads*) Hey . . Kit, you remember that joke you used to tell . . that great joke . . guy goes into a . . you know . . he . .

KIT

OK, Woody . .

EVA

Go ahead, Woody . . (*pause*)

WOODY

Ahh, it was an old joke . .

EVA

Guy goes into a whore house . . and what?

KIT

What else. Woody, you going to take a cab home from here?

WOODY

Oh . . sure. (*to Eva*) That was a great dinner, Eva . . great roast . .

EVA

Thank you.

WOODY

I'll take a bus down.

KIT

You know where that sheaf of papers is in the blue folder with the layout of this floor . . all that?

WOODY

What? (*Kit continues opening lockers*) Oh . . got me. (*to Eva*) But you know I could use a drink.

EVA

When is your probation over? (*Kit listens to them from inside the men's room*)

WOODY

Quite a while . . (*scratches*) Maybe I'll sack out here tonight. (*lies down on the table and crosses his hands over his chest; Eva puts the glass on his crossed hands*)

KIT

Sorry, kid. Can't sleep down here. This isn't the midnight mission.

WOODY

Midnight mission . . ha, ha, ha, ha, ha . . hear that? Ha, ha, ha, ha.

EVA

Ha, ha, ha.

WOODY

Kit, I just thought about when we were kids. You know . . funny, I just thought about it . . when you used to lead the gang, Kit, and . .

KIT

Come on, Woody, look, you . .

WOODY

(*to Eva*) I told you about that the other night when I was over at the apartment . . to celebrate your arrival . . what a joker he was . .

EVA

Never know it now, would you? Ha, ha, ha . . Who am I, honey? On second thought he always jokes with me. Just jokes with me . .

KIT

Ha, ha, ha . .

EVA

Reach out. (*beckons to him*) Reach out to me, honey . . (*pause*) Ha, ha, ha (*to Woody*) He doesn't even try . . not drunk enough . .

KIT

All right, Eva . .

EVA

Tonight?

WOODY

Look . . I want to thank you for having me over . . again . . and I'm sorry I dropped in so unexpectedly.

EVA

(*approaches him*) Come over any time. Any time.

WOODY

Well . .

KIT

We'll have him over again . . uh . .

EVA

Come over any time . .

WOODY

Maybe I'll take you up on that. I have to get out of my place every night down in the Village anyway . . they always have some party going on . . throwing bottles out of windows. People come into your room.

EVA

Woody, you need a good woman to take care of you, you know . . a good girl . . (*Kit is now at the lockers again*)

KIT

Woody, what's the time?

WOODY

Twelve midnight about . .

KIT

(*clearing out junk, aggravated*) This place is a garbage dump!

WOODY

I was going to get around to those, Kit . .

KIT

You were.

EVA

What time's that man coming to the apartment?

KIT

A little while.

WOODY

Who is that? What's that about?

KIT

What? (*searching a locker*)

EVA

Some animal.

WOODY

Ha, ha, ha . . you're . .

EVA

I'm what?

WOODY

You know . . Kit . . you married a beautiful girl. Beautiful. You know that . . (*to Eva*)

EVA

Of course . .

WOODY

(*to Kit*) And she's got humility . . you see. (*pulls out a pack of cigarettes*)

EVA

Oh, let me have one of those . .

WOODY

Ha, ha, ha . . again?

KIT

You . . you have to get this place cleaned up, Woody. You have to get this cleaned up.

WOODY

Match? Try the end one. (*to Eva as he sticks two cigarillos in his mouth*)

EVA

Yeah.

WOODY

How's that?

EVA

They're getting stale.

WOODY

Hell, you nearly smoked them all up.

EVA

Just put it down to my altruistic nature.

WOODY

Your what?

EVA

Helping you to cut down on your smoking . . so you won't get lung cancer.

WOODY

Ha, ha, ha . . these Spanish tobaccos are mild . .

EVA

(*yelling to Kit*) Honey? When are we going to Europe?

KIT

(*rips open the last locker — toys spill to the floor*) What? Jesus, I . .

WOODY

(*looking in*) You OK? What happened? You OK?

KIT

Look at this . . this Fibber McGee here . . throw this stuff away, will you?

WOODY

Sure. (*comes into the locker area, begins picking up the junk*)

EVA

When are we going to Europe, honey?

KIT

What? What's that you're smoking? Oh, one of Woody's.

EVA

Yeah. I'd like to go to . . to Switzerland. In high school I used to ski, you know . .

KIT

Sure. We'll go. We'll go.

EVA

You should have seen me . . I used to jump.

KIT

Ha, ha, ha . .

EVA

No! Really I did . . Mom and Dad and I went on ski trips . .

KIT

We'll get there.

EVA

When?

KIT

We'll see.

EVA

(*sullen like a child*) Never. (*just then, Woody emerges from the locker room wiping his hands*)

WOODY

Aw, you oughta go. Right now! Tonight. Run away from this place. Then you oughta go to Spain . . through La Mancha country . . down to Cádiz . . beautiful clean city . . Hell, you could take a second honeymoon.

EVA

Yes, and you can come along and be our guide . . Actually we could go on our "first" honeymoon. All we did when we got married was to stay at the parents' apartment . . (*to Kit*) Oh, honey, let's go . .

WOODY

Of course. You have to break right out. Get to Barcelona . . beautiful Gothic section . . near the waterfront . . beautiful place . . there was this incident that happened to me at . .

KIT

(*interrupting*) Well, we have to get back. We'll talk about it some other time. You going now, kid?

WOODY

Well, maybe I'll stick around for a while . . clean up the lockers . .

EVA

You come over any time you want. (*takes his hand*) You don't have to work so hard . . does he, Kit? You're not going to make him work now.

WOODY

You're the boss.

KIT

Take off. See you tomorrow morning.

EVA

Come over tomorrow night . . tell me some more of your adventures . .

WOODY

Well . . we'll . . we'll see . . Good night.

EVA

Good night . . adventurer . . Ha, ha, ha. (*kisses Woody on the cheek*)

WOODY

(*sees Kit's distaste*) See you tomorrow. (*Kit doesn't answer and Woody turns and goes up steps; pause*)

EVA

He's . . he's a very fine person, Kit . . Despite what you say about him to me.

KIT

What are you talking about? Let's go . . (*takes her arm*)

EVA

Little things you come out with . . he's irresponsible . . all that . . his version seems a little different.

KIT

And he has you believing him, of course . .

EVA

Yes, I believe him.

KIT

Yet you've known him for only . . only two days! For Christ's sake. You're drunk. Let's get back . . (*takes her arm*)

EVA

Don't steer me around. (*breaks away*) Don't . . ever do that . . Just . . don't . . I'm . . I'm . . not . . not drunk . . why do you hate him! Why do you have such . . a . . hostility.

KIT

Hate him? I don't hate him. Just because I tell you that he . . he manufactures a few things. Why, he's always been a great one for stories. You just have to take what he says with a grain of salt. That's all. (*pause*) I'm sorry if I upset you. OK? (*pause*)

EVA

I believe him . .

Scene 2

Two days later, the basement.

GRAZZO

(*takes a tremendous windup as Flesher enters via the elevator off right and throws the ball*) Strike three!

FLESHER

Yer out! (*he's sweating, annoyed*) Look, I . .

GRAZZO

You hear the game, boss?

FLESHER

(*breathing hard*) I told you to cut that crap. I told you to cut it. I'll show you who's boss! You watch that. (*pause*) Where the hell is he? What did he do with the goddamn shipment of nine thousand marbles?

GRAZZO

Woody? He's in the can.

FLESHER

Yeah? I hope he don't mistake himself and flush him down. I'm goin' to quit this dump!

GRAZZO

(*after a pause*) Hey . . did you check on it for sure upstairs . . just now?

FLESHER

Upstairs. Everybody's fulla crap here. Upstairs. Sure I checked on it. I went up there an' said I thought I was gettin' the job down here an' what d'you think about that? They looked at me like I was . . like I was somethin' stuck unner a shoe. (*pause*) I just came out of personnel. (*The toilet flushes with a roar. Whistling from the bathroom off left. Flesher advances to the men's room.*) Goddamnit! He's gonna get somethin' done here!

GRAZZO

He's been laying off the last couple of days . . keeps forgetting to sort the mail . .

FLESHER

Hey! Get outta there! What'd you fall in? Let's get rollin' here. (*no answer; whistling continues*) Come on, wise guy. (*Whistling continues. Flesher, steaming, goes and kicks open the bathroom door. Woody steps out for a moment.*)

WOODY

You want something? (*calmly*)

FLESHER

Look you. (*Woody wipes his face with a towel*) I told you about that shipment of marbles . .

WOODY

Marbles?

FLESHER

Hey you.

WOODY

Look, I'm on my break. What's your problem?

FLESHER

I don't know where you worked, wise guy, but here you only get fifteen minutes . . not forty-five. You got that?

WOODY

Why, you're coming in clear . . and loud. Why don't you relax . . have a cup of Sanka. How we doing, Grazzo? (*no answer; to Grazzo*) He's a little bugged . . (*Grazzo still is silent*) Why don't we sit down and talk it out, Bud? Civilized conversation. (*Flesher looks at him and blinks*)

FLESHER

OK, joker. OK. (*calmly*) OK, if I start?

WOODY

Shoot. Look I know you've been bothered about that rumor but it's a lot of hearsay, Bud . .

FLESHER

Look, wise guy. You been screwin' around here th' last two days. You got me up to th' neck with yer stories . . bull. You got to work or else you get th' hell outta here and pretty goddamn soon!

WOODY

Tell it to them upstairs!

FLESHER

Upstairs? Listen to him, Grazzo. Upstairs. I'll kick yer ass outta here right now if you want. You'll get outta here just like Harris went before you got here . .

GRAZZO

Yeah . . hahahahah . .

FLESHER

You don't rate upstairs, joker. You're just like us. You don't got no special privileges, y'know. What the hell you do with a bum like this? (*to Grazzo*) Takes a half hour break every five minutes . . Goofs off . .

WOODY

Look, you can't fire me . . personnel has to . .

FLESHER

Yer dreamin'. You'll go just like Harris, th' ladykiller. They'll give you a couple promises after they find out yer gone . .

GRAZZO

You'll end up in Brooklyn at th' distributor they got out there . . cleaning out the heads . . filling orders . . signing packing slips . . file clerk . . I seen him out there . . Harris . . Hell, a long time ago there was a guy saved up money down here and bought a gun. He shot himself in the head, nobody cares.

FLESHER

(*to Grazzo*) OK, OK. All I got t'make out is a little report . . and goodbye.

WOODY

(*after a moment*) OK . . what do you want me to do? Those marbles are over in the elevator. Carton needs a label.

FLESHER

Get to cleanin' off them toy racks . . elbow grease. (*Woody moves*)
Clean up th' floor here . . take care of these orders . . (*yellow slips on
the table*) Sweep th' floor down with a wet broom. We ain't shippin' dust
here. I'm goin' on my break now. (*to Grazzo*) You stay down here awhile
. . keep th' joker company . .

GRAZZO

Aw, ha, ha . . how long you gonna be onna break? I gotta get goin' with
this mail . . through rain, sleet, an' snow . . and they got Second Avenue chopped up aroun' Forty-First . .

FLESHER

I'll be across th' street at Benny's. A shipment of Giganto-puppets is
comin' in, but that should be after I get back. Big puppets . .

GRAZZO

Anything happens I'll throw them out! Hey! When you quittin' work
here?

FLESHER

Ahhh . . yer funny. (*waves at Grazzo, gives Woody a look, and goes off
right*) Don't worry about it. There'll be some fun . .

GRAZZO

Through the rain . . sleet, and snow . .

WOODY

Say, Grazzo . . what's this about Bud quitting?

GRAZZO

You oughta know. (*at this moment Eva appears on the stairs*)

EVA

Hello, Woody . . Grazzo.

GRAZZO

G'afternoon Missus Mills . . how did th' meeting turn out?

EVA

The meeting? Kit isn't out yet . .

GRAZZO

Ah . . (*pause*)

WOODY

What do you mean I ought to know? About Bud quitting . .

GRAZZO

He's quitting . . gettin' another job. He didn't get th' job down here like
you said! He found out from personnel. They didn't know what the hell
he was talking about . . an' you build it up in his head . .

WOODY

WHAT?

GRAZZO

Yeah? You shoulda seen him th' last couple nights th' way he was talking! You really had him believin' that he . . he was gonna become head of th' basement.

WOODY

Wait . . wait a minute . . they turned him down? Why?

GRAZZO

They didn't know what he was talkin' about. They didn't turn him down . . they didn't even consider him . . that's th' way they work . . well, I knew it all th' time . . that he wasn't gonna become head of th' basement.

EVA

Oh yes . . there's a man named . . Steele or something.

WOODY

Steele? Who's he? Look . . are you sure about this? I mean . . Kit told me that . .

EVA

Remember a couple of nights ago when we were down here, Woody? Remember Kit had to go see a man that night . . that was Steele, he . .

WOODY

But . . Kit didn't tell me about that. He never said a word about . . somebody else coming in and taking the job.

EVA

Big deal . .

WOODY

It so happens it is a big deal! Why in the hell did Kit tell me Flesher was getting his job? He . . You've heard him say that, Grazzo. You've heard it . .

GRAZZO

Aaah . . he kids around with Bud . . they joke around. Mister Mills knows Bud has a deal coming up with Corning Glass . .

WOODY

But Flesher believed it . .

GRAZZO

Only when you . . when you build it up . . I mean somebody tells you somethin' . . OK. It's a joke . . but when two guys they tell you th' same thing . . then you believe it . . y'know . . (*pause*)

115

WOODY

He wasn't kidding him, Grazzo. I can tell when Kit fools around . .
I've known him awhile, you know. Looks to me more like placating . .
like Flesher's got some great power over Kit . . It was like Kit really
meant it . .

EVA

Flesher will get over it. He'll quit here . . go to Corning Glass like
Grazzo says . .

GRAZZO

(*after pause*) Well . . I gotta take off. See you at four . . Nice seein'
you agin, Missus Mills . .

EVA

Good-bye. (*Grazzo slings mailbag over his shoulder and moves off right*)
Woody . . how come you haven't come over to the apartment?

WOODY

What? Oh . .

EVA

You said you'd come over again . .

WOODY

Why should I? I've been busy . . You know . . your husband acts
like he needs votes to stay alive around here . .

EVA

Maybe he does. (*pause*) He needs something . . You . .

WOODY

(*interrupting*) Look . . I'm . . I'm sorry but I have a lot of work to do
. .

EVA

I won't get in your way . . I'll just wait here for the meeting to break . .

WOODY

Suit yourself.

EVA

OK. (*sits behind the table, watches him*) Got any more of those cigarillos?

WOODY

No.

EVA

No — Yes?

WOODY

I'm not in the mood. (*throws dolls in carton*)

EVA

Are you moody? I love moody people. I'm moody myself, you know . .

ha, ha, ha . . say you're very very good at wrapping dolls . . Bet you're just as good at unwrapping them . . (*pause*)

WOODY

(*stops, looks at her*) Why don't you wait upstairs?

EVA

The old heave-ho, eh?

WOODY

Look . .

EVA

Well, I'm probably leaving this place soon enough anyway. Just as soon as that meeting is up and I find out again . . that your brother is hung up here . . like last time. They held the same kind of meeting before . . the usual situation, but I told him . . I told him this morning that I was going for good this time. I have some money. I'll take a little trip to Europe . . those places you've been, love. Oh, Kit and I had a hell of a fight this morning . . nice healthy fight . .

WOODY

You ought to take it easy with him . .

EVA

You care? Why, you influenced me . . I want to get to . . to Spain, North Africa. God, when I was in college . . before I flunked out, that is . . all the girls had been to Europe. You know . . their first affair in some greasy gondola . . romance. But here . . in this country everybody always looks up your dress. (*pokes him*)

WOODY

Do you . . you care about him at all? How can you . . I mean . .

EVA

What are you talking about? Yes, of course . . but I can't keep it up . . fighting a desert. Yes, but I am like a . . a plaything to him . . An object . . at one time I thought maybe he had some other women . . you know . . something as banal as all that, but he is disgustingly honest, you know . . at least about being faithful. (*pause*) I can't figure out what it is with him, what keeps him away from me . .

WOODY

Away from you? You seem to be leaving him . .

EVA

Oh, you're just seeing nowadays. You don't know the old me . . of a year ago. When I played the old game with Kit . . Oh, I wanted a little baby, after three years of marriage . . I wanted to have my own baby . . well, I don't know what happened. He . . he was disgusted . .

117

suddenly the old joking stopped . . zero . . I don't know what happened.
WOODY
So that's why you . . when I found you at the station, you . . (*stops*)
EVA
What?
WOODY
You weren't exactly turning that bum down . .
EVA
What the hell if I wasn't . . Don't give me that kind of a look, honey. What are you? Mister Clean? You . . have no idea what was going on . . he talked to me . . not like I was some . . object. He . . it was the way I thought . . If I had a drink maybe I'd leave this basement. Go back to the apartment. To a movie . . (*she is nervously agitated*)
WOODY
You OK?
EVA
Nervous. You know we feel the same way about Kit. You're the one who said he needs votes to stay alive . . Oh, anything but yours truly I guess. But you know I've gotten to the point where sometimes I just don't care. I come back here from California after waiting for him to come out . . and he gives me the big hello . . which is followed by the truth which is . . the same old thing . . Here we are . . here we must stay! And God damn it, he knows I can't stay here! He must . . he must just hate me . . Woody . . My God . .
WOODY
Why can't you stay here . . ?
EVA
Kit knows. But, I'm telling you, I've . . I've tried to move to him . . The more I move to him, he moves away. He runs away from me. (*pause*) There . . there just has to be an ultimatum; a payoff. And that's today. My God, I just don't see any other way . .
WOODY
Take it easy . .
EVA
I'm sorry . . I'm just . . I'll be all right . .
WOODY
You're shaking . . take it easy . .
EVA
I'll be OK . . if I had a drink or something . .

WOODY

I guess you do need one . . (*pause*) Look . . why don't you sit there . . I just remembered that Grazzo keeps a bottle here . . Bourbon. In the toy cash registers. You partial to Bourbon? . .

EVA

Anything . .

WOODY

Sure . . take it easy . . (*He goes off left behind the racks. There is a no sale ring of the cash register. Woody appears with a bottle.*) OK . . still some left . . sorry no ice.

EVA

(*takes the bottle, takes a swig*) UGGH . . (*horrible face*) Great . . you take it. Is it still good?

WOODY

(*takes bottle, drinks, spills it down his front*) Not bad . . you know how long it's been since I had a drink? Nine years . . you feel better? (*she takes the bottle again*)

EVA

(*drinking*) I will . . you make me feel . . you make me feel great, Woody. (*pause*) I'm sorry . . don't want to give you the wrong impression about me . . You spilled the drink, you slob.

WOODY

Yes. Excuse me. I better get out of this before Kit gets down . . (*She is up and wiping him with his own T-shirt. Her hands move the shirt sensuously over his body.*)

EVA

You're just like a little boy . .

WOODY

(*takes shirt, moves away*) I don't get this . . this intensity you have about this place . . You don't explode out of your mind over some dump . . I don't see it.

EVA

Well, Kit knows . . (*then tossing it off*) Oh, you know . . I'm from the west coast . . suburbia. I originally came out here with my old man. Big push to get me married. I was spending more time hanging out in joints around school than I was in a classroom. Guess I didn't take to anything they had on the menu . . (*pause*) Mom and Dad brought me here for a kind of change of atmosphere . . So, one day I was in the Automat, you see, and I see this . . I see Kit staring at me. I wasn't wearing anything revealing you know, but there he was . . holding a tray and staring . .

he looked frightened. (*pause*) He . . he came right over to the table I was sitting at, and he parked himself in front of me . . staring . . scared the hell out of me, you know? You know what the first thing was that he said to me . . He said . . "Haven't been doing too much the last few years . ." That's what he said. No "Hello . . may I join you?" . . just "I haven't been doing too much the last few years." That really hit me, Woody. I mean . . that really knocked me out. (*remembers*) I remember how it was outside. Raining and there was a mist rising from the streets. It was after the dinner hour . . not so packed, but I felt some kind . . of pressure in the Automat . . hell, maybe the sandwich doors would suddenly . . you know . . fly open and reveal something horrible . . that's what I felt like. Anyway, he didn't talk too much after that, but we met again . . and finally he took me out. Took me out to the beach . . (*Woody moves his head*) Out on the beach. He didn't say anything to me there either. I did feel better out there though. One day Mom and Dad left town to go home, and we were married.

WOODY

He — he took you out to the beach . . Where?

EVA

Oh . . out near Atlantic City . .

WOODY

Asbury Park . .

EVA

Yes . . (*pause*) You've been out there?

WOODY

A long time ago . . (*remembering*)

EVA

That's where I felt . . I felt . . you know . . out in the open. (*sipping from bottle*) Everything was OK then . . in a way . . but . . gradually . . (*Woody takes another drink*) Oh, my parents left . . left . . and things started to fall apart on this end . . (*pause*) but . . you've been thinking about something else while I've been talking . .

WOODY

Oh . . no . .

EVA

You daydream, don't you?

WOODY

Who doesn't.

EVA

Tell me something . . have you a girl?

WOODY

Yes.

EVA

You must have lots of them . .

WOODY

No, only one. (*pause*)

EVA

Oh . .

WOODY

Just Ann.

EVA

Well . . tell me something about her.

WOODY

(*testily*) Why?

EVA

Is she pretty?

WOODY

Beautiful.

EVA

She as beautiful as you said I was?

WOODY

What?

EVA

When we were down here two nights ago . . you told me I was beautiful
. . (*comes toward him*) Remember?

WOODY

(*pause*) I thought you were interested in what a man thought of a woman's
mind. In a man . . talking to a woman . . Why, Ann has the most
beautiful mind.

EVA

Ha, ha, ha. (*Voices are heard above the steps as Eva takes his arm and
moves to him. The voices come closer. Kit's voice is heard.*)

KIT'S VOICE

Is she gone?

FLESHER'S VOICE

Wrapped it up now, eh?

WOODY

(*shaking her arm off*) Somebody's coming down . . (*footsteps on stairs;
Eva turns*)

121

EVA

Woody. (*urgently*) Listen, Woody . . If it's the same old thing, I . .

WOODY

TAKE IT EASY!

EVA

Kit . .

KIT

Uh . . hello, honey . . Bud told me you came down. (*pause*)

EVA

Anything . . happen? What happened?

KIT

(*puts his arm around her*) Hello, pigeon . . ha, ha, ha . . little meeting. Routine . . policy (*looks around at Flesher who is examining whiskey bottle*) Everything's OK . . everything's fine . . Come down to pay me a little visit.

FLESHER

Looks like a party down here . . (*holds up bottle*)

EVA

You . . you mean then . . we're goin' . . then? We're going?

WOODY

(*forced joviality*) She was really worried, Kit.

KIT

Worried? Everything's fine. Just fine . . er . . why don't you run along home. I'll be in about six . . we'll have dinner out . . a little talk. Put on that blue sack thing, ha, ha, ha. OK?

EVA

Honey . .

KIT

(*squeezes her slightly*) Run along now . . we have to get cracking here. Bud, take her up . . get her a cab. (*pulls out money and gives it to Flesher*) Tough to get a cab this time of day.

EVA

It's . . we're really going. (*Kit nods slightly. She goes to him, kisses him, then goes up with Flesher. Speaks as she goes*) You coming in at six? Oh Kit . . I . . (*relieved*) I'm very happy . . (*Kit watches her as she goes up with Flesher*)

WOODY

Well, that's great. Really great, Kit. Man . .

KIT

(*looks at bottle*) Doing a little celebrating here, eh?

WOODY

(*slapping Kit on back*) I'm glad everything worked out for you. Hell, I knew you'd get out of here.

KIT

(*pause*) Yeah. (*looks Woody over*) Christ! I can smell you from here.

WOODY

Ha, ha, ha . . you see . . she . .

KIT

You're supposed to lay off that stuff aren't you? What in God's name is wrong with you? (*goes over to table*) Look at this . . this mess here? This . . (*picks yellow packing slips up from table*) You, you have no control. I am convinced you just have no control . . just look at this place.

WOODY

What? (*quizzically looking at Kit*) Now . .

KIT

(*at bottle again*) Where in the hell did this come from? (*pauses, looks at edge, wipes finger around the edge, looks at finger*)

WOODY

Look . . uh . . Eva had a taste . . she was nervous about the meeting . . she was waiting for you, talking about you.

KIT

What the hell was she doing down here? Little tête-à-tête, as they say? Why didn't she wait upstairs? She could have done that, you know.

WOODY

(*after pause*) Kit . . what's .

KIT

WHY didn't she wait upstairs? For God's sake . .

WOODY

Well . . she was . .

KIT

You gave her a little talk . . a few drinks . . stories . .

WOODY

(*angrily*) Kit. For Christ's sake. You're constructing a whole . . big deal. What's with you? (*Kit throws bottle in corner where it shatters. He then moves about restlessly, stops, reaches into wallet, removes card, looks at it and stands.*) Look . . I mean . . I have an idea . . Why don't I take you out to dinner tonight. You and me, Kit. We'll take in a show . . Anything you wish . . It's on me. I'll — we'll celebrate.

KIT

Forget it. Just . . forget it . . (*pause*) I'm not going away yet. They suspended the transfer for another week . . week and a walk. (*pause as Woody looks in disbelief*)

WOODY

Are you . . are you kidding?

KIT

Of course not. I don't blame them because . .

WOODY

Just now? (*pause*)

KIT

Yes. That's right.

WOODY

(*pause*) I can't believe it . . did you say anything?

KIT

Look, I don't want to talk about it . .

WOODY

But . . you told Eva . . you lied to her, Kit . . you . .

KIT

(*angrily*) It's none of your goddamn business. Who asked you to stick your face in it. Who asked you. What right do you have to . . (*he stops*) She'll be OK . . I can handle her, I can handle her. (*Woody steps back; pause*) Uh . . I get a raise in pay. A new position when I get to the coast. I'll be selling for the company with a good commission . . big salary. Practically my own hours. Oh . . she'll enjoy the money when it starts to come in . . (*pause*) She'll enjoy it . . they've promised me many attractive values . . I could never get them here.

WOODY

They've . . they've promised you . .

KIT

Yes . .

WOODY

You know . . it sounds like . . well, Grazzo was telling me about . . you remember Harris . .

KIT

(*remembrance*) Harris . . (*bitterness*) What does he have to do with it?

WOODY

Grazzo told me they promised him plenty . . but they have him out in Brooklyn . . at the distributor . . Grazzo saw him pulling crap detail . . filling orders in the basement still . .

KIT

Well . . he . . well, certainly. He had his chance here . . everybody
gets their chance, kid . . some people don't work out . . but they go
to other jobs. It's no great crime not to work out in a place . . he just
didn't fit in here . . you must remember that if a person doesn't work out
. . it's nothing bad . . all they want upstairs is their due. You see . .
(*last part personalized to Woody*)

WOODY

What?

KIT

Well, Bud has come to me . .

WOODY

Well . . I . . I don't see.

KIT

We had a talk after the meeting . . upstairs . . About my job . . I . .
I get the idea from him that you built up some story in his mind that he was
to get my job down here, you see?

WOODY

Some story? Why, you told him that yourself. You said it here. Grazzo
heard you tell Flesher he was getting your job.

KIT

Woody, you don't seem to understand. You manufacture this . . a kind
of joke Flesher and I play . . an understanding we have . . into a
reality for the man. He never took it seriously from me. Grazzo knows
it was a joke. Doesn't he? (*pause*) Well, doesn't he?

WOODY

I don't see it that way, Kit. You . . you never joked around like that
. . I think he really expected to get the job . . you see . . I don't see
that I would have convinced him . . because if he really knew that he
wasn't getting it, then . . I mean, I get the feeling that Flesher thinks
you owe it to him, Kit. (*pause*) I think he expected to really get it from
you . .

KIT

Owe it to him? How . . how could I owe him anything? Say, that's not
logical . . you're way off base, kid. Way off. Oh, you convinced him all
right. It all comes down to . . to a natural ability you have . . A salesman would give his right arm to have the gift of gab you have. You know
. . I can remember a dozen times. More . . When you were in high
school debates . . Hell, you took the forensic medal for debates for the
sophomore class and junior and senior . . (*pause*) Woody, you under-

125

stand . . (*taking Woody into his confidence, it seems*) These men down here . . they're simple people . . they work completely on emotion, not logic. Of course it's logical that Bud couldn't get my job . . that's — but his brain doesn't connect that way . . the way I look at it . . I think you have to be involved with a higher type of personality . . You know what I mean . . I don't think this place is for you . . And . . I really think you feel shut up here . . You know what I mean, don't you?

WOODY

Look, what do you want to tell me? You don't have to sugar it up with me, Kit. You want me to apologize to Flesher . . You want me to uh . . pat him on the back . . take him out for a drink . . clean up the men's room . . I mean . . just call it, Kit. You don't have to appease me, you know . . Not me. (*Flesher enters*)

FLESHER

She got off OK . .

KIT

Oh . . uh . .

FLESHER

That shipment of Giganto-puppets got here . . You want me to load it on the dolly?

KIT

Right . . right. (*Flesher goes off*)

WOODY

Kit . .

KIT

OK, kid . . OK . . Tomorrow morning . . I want you to put on your suit. Take a trip out to Kew Gardens . . You've been out there . .

WOODY

Sure . . when we were kids you took me . . showed me how to peg a ball out there . . I remember that place very well . . you want me to pick up some orders? I'll get out there first thing in the morning . .

KIT

No, kid. (*takes out card he had in his hand before, gives it to Woody*) Here . .

WOODY

Al Grey . . used cars? I don't get it.

KIT

You remember Al, kid. One of Dad's old friends . .

126

WOODY

Oh . . Yeah, yeah . . I do. Big guy with a yellow vest . . He used to wear a yellow vest. He always had sandwiches in his pockets . .

KIT

Right . .

WOODY

Sure, I remember him . .

KIT

He was very fond of you. Used to bring you a present every time he came over . . I had a talk with him. He called about a week ago all of a sudden. He asked about you . . said he had gotten in the used car business . . he said he needed some salesmen . . Somebody who could talk . . talk to people . . you know what I mean . . Good commission . . meeting people . .

WOODY

Well, so . .

KIT

Woody, how would you like to be a used car salesman? A car salesman. Out in the open in a lot.

WOODY

What, are you kidding? . . What do you mean, Kit?

KIT

Uh . . kid, I think you should go out to Al and talk about being . . about working as a salesman. Funny thing . . I knew it was for you when he called. The perfect job for you.

WOODY

You're kidding! What should I want to go out there for? What is this.

KIT

Look . .

WOODY

Look what. What the hell are you doing?

KIT

I'm sorry. You have to take the job, kid.

WOODY

Jesus . .

KIT

It's perfect for you. Out in the open . . talking to people . . It's . .

WOODY

You mean . .

127

KIT

Sounds like the thing . . just for you . . You know Al and . . Well, you have the golden words . . You've always . .

WOODY

You're firing me then. You're firing me . . that's what you've been . . beating around with . . ?

KIT

Woody.

WOODY

Out, eh? That's it? Out?

KIT

It's not . . it's not that way. It's . .

WOODY

Why? Why? You . .

KIT

I'm trying to give you what the hell you really want, kid. Better job, more pay, out in the air . . where you can talk to people . . a perfect job for you.

WOODY

What I want? That right? That what I want? Why the hell are you doing this? Because of a little friction down here. That's your answer to the big friction . . You make me sick! (*tears up card and throws it*) SICK! Well . . that's really something. I have to take the job . . I *have* to take it . . Jesus . .

KIT

Woody, I . .

WOODY

You what. What the hell.

KIT

I told you because things don't work out here it is nothing to . .

WOODY

What things, what! Flesher? You know he's got some deal with Corning Glass . . He can go over there. He's quitting as a matter of fact and you know about that. Grazzo said you knew about that like everything else . . Where the hell's your so-called friction then? It's gone.

KIT

That's . . that's part of it. Flesher's only part of it.

WOODY

What does that mean?

KIT

Flesher himself . . he's not the issue. What I've been saying is that you would . . you can't help yourself when it comes to building stories in somebody's mind is what I mean. Flesher . . Eva . . yourself . . anybody who might come along . . anybody . .

WOODY

Eva . . Well . . I . .

KIT

You know . . she . . she came to me today . . said she'd leave . . she said she'd go to Europe. Your words came out of her mouth, Woody. Your exact words . . like a record. It's funny . . It's just a matter of coincidence . . You coming here . . and Eva being in one of her childish moods the last few weeks . . She's so young . . Feels like I treat her like a doll you know . . like one of the toys down here . . Perhaps that added to the potency of . . running away . . made it into a reality for her . . Now she would come to you for support, and she would draw it from you like a sponge . . Misconstrue whatever you might say to fit her own mood . . You see what I mean.

WOODY

Kit . . I . . I don't think so. I mean . . I don't think she'd just run out . . She . . She couldn't mean it.

KIT

Woody . . Listen . . I just want to avoid it. I just want to keep it from happening . . because she works strictly from emotion. She dreams . . I have to keep her, kid. I . . I love her very much . . and sometimes . . I get so alone without her around . . I feel like everything is . . torn away from me . .

WOODY

Kit . . (*sympathy*)

KIT

You, you can help me. You can really help me.

WOODY

How ?

KIT

Take the job. It's a good job, and I know you'll do well. It's the start for you, believe me. This place. It gets to you. Presses in, and it's like hell for you, isn't it? I don't want to crush this gift you have.

WOODY

Kit, how long can you keep her in a closet . . You can't keep running away from . . Well, from what she is . . She's . .

KIT

No . . no . . It'll be touch and go for a while . . true . . now that they've canceled me again, but I understand her mind. I know her very well. She'll come out of it. You know, Dorothea's mind worked the same way . . dreaming . . impulsive . . She was impulsive . . Don't you think Dad must have appeared like . . like a great man to Dorothea . . coming from the Midwest like she did? He had her in the palm of his hand . . and we never knew it . . until suddenly he married her . . A fifty-year-old man . . and she was so young . . so beautiful . . He just . . suddenly married her . .

FLESHER

Comin' through! Comin' through! (*wheels a large carton onstage*) Phil came in . .

KIT

What? Yes, thank . . you . .

FLESHER

(*rips open carton*) OK. OK. One at a time.

KIT

(*to Woody*) He'll be expecting you at nine in the morning . . out at the car lot . .

FLESHER

Look at this will you? (*Kit leaves Woody standing alone as the curtain falls*)

ACT THREE

Scene 1

Next day, lunch hour, the basement. Grazzo and Flesher are eating their lunches. A large puppet is on the table. At rise, the scene holds, then the elevator sounds.

FLESHER

Who is that? Didn't you hang out th' lunch hour sign? What'd you forget again? Where's yer head.

GRAZZO

Yeah, I hung out th' sign. Boss!

FLESHER

Don't start that again I told you . .

GRAZZO

(*sniffing the air*) Smells like old socks . .

FLESHER

(*holding up a huge pair of shears used for ripping boxes*) Come 'ere, I'll cut yer nose off . .

GRAZZO

(*looking off right as elevator stops*) Hey . . hey, Woody. (*Woody enters in a suit and tie*)

WOODY

Hello . . (*he is embarrassed*)

GRAZZO

Hey looka th' threads . . Y'got yer little suit on.

WOODY

Yeah. Kit around?

FLESHER

He'll be back after lunch. You want to give him a message?

WOODY

Oh . . he called me . . said he wanted me to come down in the lunch hour . .

GRAZZO

Said he wouldn't be back fer a while . .

FLESHER

Yeah. He said if you showed up to clean yer stuff outta th' locker, an' he left this. (*pulls envelope from his pocket*)

WOODY

What's that? I thought he'd be here . .

FLESHER

(*gives Woody the envelope*) Maybe it's a note fer ya.

WOODY

I wanted to talk to him about . . (*pulls out a W-2 form, pink slip, and check*)

FLESHER

Why, looka that. It's yer termination. (*after a moment*) Uh . . Hey . . Woody. Ann's been callin' ya on th' phone. Yer girl friend. I talked t'her. (*pause*) I told her you'd probably be around. She'll call back.

WOODY

What? Oh . . yeah . . (*pause*) Ann?

GRAZZO

Yeah.

WOODY

Well . . Jesus . . Kit didn't say anything . . (*Flesher shakes his head. Woody stuffs the envelope in his pocket.*) Look . . uh . . I'll . . I'll

131

come here tonight . . pick up my stuff from the locker . . (*starts away*)
Thanks . . Thank you . .

FLESHER

Whattaya want me to tell th' girl? What about yer girl? I'll tell her t'meet
you here tonight . . how about that?

WOODY

Yes. Tell her about ten. Good-bye.

GRAZZO

Hey, listen. Come around. Say hello an' — you know. Come down an' have
a cupa Sanka an' a donut . . tell us what yer doing.

WOODY

Sure. Thanks . . (*exit*)

FLESHER

S'long sports fans . . (*pause*)

GRAZZO

(*looks after Woody*) Sure . . Hey, when I answered the phone earlier,
that broad didn't sound like Ann.

FLESHER

Ha, ha, ha . . (*claps his hands together*) We're gonna have us some
party.

GRAZZO

Wha'?

FLESHER

T'night. We're gonna give Woody a goin' away party. Be my goin' away
too, y'know . . remember what I told ya about Considine over at Corning Glass? I got me a job over there any time I wanna start after a week.
They can take this hole and shove it.

GRAZZO

Ya got it, hah?

FLESHER

Sure. Well, we'll really have a party t'night.

GRAZZO

Yeah . . I'll tell you somethin' . . secretly I feel kinda sorry fer
Woody. He wasn't such a bad head.

FLESHER

Ahh, whattaya talkin'? Him an' his brother'r both bastards, each in his
own way o'course. Why, Kit did th' same damn thing when he thought
Harris was foolin' around with his wife. He canned him, didn't he?

GRAZZO

Yeah. That's a fact. Booooy, I'll never forget that night when old Kit

came in drunk after findin' them . . Remember that? What th' hell did
he say? Somethin' about . .

FLESHER

(*pulls money from his pocket*) Listen, you get a cake, see. Coconut. Here's
a buck. (*pause, silence*)

GRAZZO

Y'know . . somebody oughta invent something like . . like a rubber
woman. Outta rubber, y'know? Hey, I'd get me one of them. Y'get a
bicycle pump, see, and you fill it up with air an' there she is . . an'
everybody gets one, an' they all look th' same . . an' maybe everything
evens off like that . . or maybe you could fill it with warm water, an'
then there you are . . ain't you?

FLESHER

What are you? A queer? (*phone rings*) Ten tonight, right!

Scene 2

The basement before ten that night. The stage is dark.

FLESHER

(*on phone, talking to Kit*) Yeah, well you better get down here. I think
someone's breaking in.

GRAZZO

(*has a mask on, and stumbles into the red light of the basement*) He's
comin'. I seen him on a street nexta Phil's bar.

FLESHER

(*also wearing a mask*) Ssssshhhh. Fer Chrissake. I got Kit on the phone.
(*in phone*) Yeah — right now.

GRAZZO

I can't breathe in this thing.

FLESHER

(*grabs Grazzo's face*) What the hell! You forgot to unplug the goddamn
nose holes.

GRAZZO

Almost killed myself on th' stairs . .

FLESHER

Listen, you turn off th' circuit breaker . .

GRAZZO

Yeah. (*Flesher flips the wall switch: no lights*) No lights . .

133

FLESHER

OK. Now here's the plan. (*grabs Grazzo's head and pulls him over*) When he comes down we'll wait until I give th' signal an' then we take this. Looks like Kit. (*Flesher holds up Giganto-puppet*)

GRAZZO

Yeah, just like him.

FLESHER

And scare th' hell outta him. Right. Then you give him the cake what you brung.

GRAZZO

What's th' signal? Wha' about . . ally ally oxen freeeee . .

FLESHER

(*clamping his hand over Grazzo's face*) Shuddup. (*noise upstairs*)

GRAZZO

Hey . . I think I heard somethin' . . What . . I need another drink . .

FLESHER

(*Grazzo clings to him*) Shhhh . . Come on. (*pulls him out of the light*)

GRAZZO

Hey . . I just thought . . What about th' broad comin' down to meet him? Remember she called an' you told her . .

FLESHER

Don't sweat it. Shhh . . quiet . .

GRAZZO

What's taken him so long?

FLESHER

Shhhh . .

GRAZZO

Christ. I stuck my hand in the cake . . (*licks his finger*) Not bad.

FLESHER

Will ya be quiet.

GRAZZO

Why're we here? (*There are footsteps, and Woody enters. He carries a suitcase with foreign labels. Wanders around the basement and sits.*)

EVA'S VOICE

Woody? (*Woody starts, looks up the stairs*) Woody? You here?

WOODY

Yeah?

EVA

(*comes down the stairs*) Turn on the lights. Can't see a damn thing.

WOODY

Eva?

EVA

Yeah. Turn on the lights.

WOODY

They must have burned out. I'll get this one. (*turns on light in men's room*)

EVA

My God, I almost got killed out there. Tripped over a garbage can or something. Ran my stocking. Great day for all concerned. Look at that. (*extends her leg, looks at him*) What's the matter?

WOODY

What are you doing down here?

EVA

What? You invited me to meet you here . . at ten . . Sorry I'm late . .

WOODY

What?

EVA

Flesher told me over the phone when I called here this afternoon. Also . .

WOODY

You called . .

EVA

Well, yes . . I pretended I was Ann over the phone . . (*Woody shakes his head*) But of course you were out . .

WOODY

My nemesis.

EVA

That's some greeting. (*pause*) Flesher in his usual manner . . told me you had been fired . . That Kit had turned you out.

WOODY

Well . .

EVA

I'm fed up to the nose with him. Fed Up. I suppose you were irresponsible or some *excuse*.

WOODY

Look . .

EVA

Some one of his excuses . .

WOODY

You have it wrong. He didn't fire me . . Actually I've been thinking of

135

leaving this place for a while . . There was a better job so . . well, it was my request to go.

EVA

You don't have to snow me, Woody . . Where the hell did he transfer you? He always transfers the people he fires . .

WOODY

It's better for me . . you have it all wrong, he . .

EVA

Where? Where did he transfer you?

WOODY

Selling cars. As a matter of fact I sold one this afternoon.

EVA

(*sardonically*) Great.

WOODY

Wasn't bad. Surprised the hell out of me. I'll make a go of it. (*pause*) Where's Kit?

EVA

Another meeting . . with Steele. Doesn't even know I'm gone, you know. He thinks I've gone to a movie or something . . I don't know . . (*Woody begins to clean out his locker*) That reminds me of my locker at school . . They never cleaned them out. When I left I stuck a tuna sandwich in my locker . . I'll bet it's still there . . When I go back home, I'll look . . (*Woody gives her a look, puts things in a suitcase*) Aren't you interested about why I called you here this afternoon?

WOODY

No.

EVA

I'll tell you anyway.

WOODY

Why don't you save your breath?

EVA

Damn, are you salty. Where's your sense of . . adventure? Some adventurer . . No curiosity . . Well. I got this . . (*holds up ticket*) Greyhound . . That's right.

WOODY

A . . ticket . . Bus ticket? (*serious*)

EVA

Yes.

WOODY

You mean you're taking off out of here . . but . .

136

EVA

I'm not going around the block.

WOODY

What the hell are you doing? You can't do that.

EVA

No?

WOODY

Are you kidding? You can't do that . . to him. I don't believe it.

EVA

You must know me better than that.

WOODY

You . . you really mean it don't you? (*she nods*) You out of your mind? You crazy? He'll . . Jesus . . How can you even . .

EVA

Do you know how I had to find out we weren't going this time? I had to call this goddamn dump. That's how. Now you were standing right here in this basement when he said we were going! Is that right? Is it?

WOODY

Eva . .

EVA

You're goddamn right he said it. He . . he . . It made me sick this morning . . Just sick . . The lies. And I couldn't talk to him this evening. I just . . I just had to get out of there. I was sick . . (*pause*) So, I guess we've both been fired.

WOODY

Listen . .

EVA

Yes.

WOODY

Well, what if he had told you the truth, Eva . . you told him then . . I think he felt that he had no choice . . but that he wanted to keep you so badly . . at least until he got you alone . . to explain that . . that things would work out . . Because he loves you very much.

EVA

What the hell is wrong with him, then? What? You know him. What in God's name is bothering him? I mean . . like you said . . he's placating. He can't stand up for himself . . What can I . . I do? Stick it out you say . . Force this feeling I have . . that I'm dead weight . . Force this feeling down? (*pause; no answer*) What? You don't know . . (*pause*) If he wants me . . He can come and get me, you know . .

WOODY

I guess he will.

EVA

You really think so? I don't .

WOODY

He will.

EVA

What are you going to do? More traveling? You're not going to stay at that car lot . .

WOODY

Why not? You know . . my adventures weren't really so great. Perhaps I did build them up. It was running that I was doing . . and I was lost most of the places I went . . Gibraltar, Paris . . Spain . . You find no home ground . . and then being in jail . . I don't know.

EVA

You think you'll stay there then . . selling.

WOODY

Yes.

EVA

Selling out.

WOODY

No. It's good for me . . I'll get a place . . get a car when my probation period is up. I'll just take it easy . .

EVA

Oh, I don't think so . .

WOODY

(*packing more into his case*) We'll see.

EVA

Bet you don't last a month out there . . Bet?

WOODY

(*moves away*) I'll make a go of it.

EVA

(*as he picks up his suitcase*) You . . you going now?

WOODY

Good-bye.

EVA

Woody . . Wait . . Please . . Don't go right . . right this second . . Please . . You don't have to go . . this minute . . (*pause*) Don't leave me right now . . I . . Please . . I don't want to stay here by myself . . I have an hour before the bus leaves.

WOODY

I don't think you better stay here.

EVA

Yes . . not by myself . .

WOODY

No . . look, Kit knows I came down here to move my stuff . . He . .

EVA

Give me one of your cigarettes. You don't have to go right now. He won't come down . . There's a meeting I told you . . Talk to me . . You better light it . . Maybe this will be the last time I see you.

WOODY

Yes.

EVA

You can stay a while . .

WOODY

Work tomorrow.

EVA

Just a few minutes then.

WOODY

A few minutes . . (*smokes*)

EVA

Yes . . I think we've both been fired . . I'm sorry I'm such a nemesis . . Really, I suppose you're mine too . . In a way. You don't think he'll ever come out to the coast, do you?

WOODY

I do think he will . .

EVA

Oh . . no . . He's flat on his behind here. Stuck. Here we are . . the two outcasts . . Here together . . all alone.

WOODY

Come on out of it. I'll get you a cab . .

EVA

Nobody knows we're here . .

WOODY

What do you say . . Let's go.

EVA

You said . . a couple of minutes . . Why don't you take off that tie?

The vein in your forehead is sticking out . . What if your head exploded
. . (*opening his shirt*) Tell me something, Woody . .

WOODY

What?

EVA

Now . . just tell me . . Don't get upset or . . or mad . . I just want
to know . . (*pause*) I just want to know . . Did . . did you ever want
to make love to me? Please . . tell me.

WOODY

Let's get out of here.

EVA

You avoid the question . . In the last week . . did you ever want to?

WOODY

No.

EVA

No, please . . didn't . . don't I appeal to you . . I mean . . your in-
stincts . . You know . . Don't I turn you on?

WOODY

I'm afraid you're not my type.

EVA

Not your type?

WOODY

I never liked it offered on a silver platter.

EVA

Oh . . touché.

WOODY

You ready to go now?

EVA

You like to chase . .

WOODY

Come on.

EVA

Ha, ha, ha. Why don't you turn off that light . . You can chase the hell
out of me . . (*Woody pushes her away, shakes her*)

WOODY

I told you it's no scene. *Come out of it. I don't want any. You get that
now?*

EVA

Oh . .

WOODY

Now stop acting like Miss Slut and let's get out of here.

EVA

OK . . OK . .

WOODY

Christ.

EVA

OK . . I . . I need a minute . . give me a minute to . . to fix my face.

WOODY

Get going.

EVA

A minute. (*She goes into the men's room. Noises, one of a doll saying "Mama." Woody moves to guard the men's room. Grazzo stands behind the Giganto-puppet.*)

WHISPERING VOICE

Help . . help . .

WOODY

Who . . Who is that? Bud?

WHISPERING VOICE

Help . . Who are you? What're you doing here?

WOODY

Bud? OK, what's the gag . .

WHISPERING VOICE

Help . . (*Grazzo pushes Giganto-puppet at Woody; it falls to floor*)
Wee, it's God . . (*laughs*)

WOODY

(*as puppet rolls near him*) Jesus . . What the hell . . OK . . What's the gag here.

WHISPERING VOICE

He, he, he . . (*Woody moves to the men's room area*)

WOODY

Eva, stay in there . .

EVA

Woody . . what . .

FLESHER

(*gets on table and roars*) Aaaaaaaaaaaaauuuuuuuuuuuugggggggggggg!!!
. . ha, ha, ha . .

WOODY

OK. What the hell is the gag. (*Flesher gives him flashlight in face*)

141

FLESHER

Death . . blood . . moider . . hee, hee, hee . . Th' spirit of Christmas past . . hee, hee.

GRAZZO

Singing in a terrible voice.

We're sorry to see youse leave.

We're sorry to see youse go.

He carries cake as he approaches.

But when you gotta go, you gotta go.

So take it easy, it's been nice

Jokin' with youse once or maybe twice.

Happy boithday to you,

Happy boithday to you,

Happy boith —

FLESHER

(*clamping his hand over Grazzo's mouth*) Awright, cut it!

GRAZZO

Hey, Woody. We brung ya a present fer yer goin' away. SURPRISE!

WOODY

Well, ha, ha, ha . . I . . Yeah . .

FLESHER

Yeah. Surprise. We just, uh . . came down here . . didn't we, Grazzo?

GRAZZO

Wha'?

FLESHER

We thought maybe there was some crooks or bums down here . . we hear some talkin' . . didn't think you'd got here yet. Right, Grazzo? (*nudges him*) Then we heard you an' Ann . .

GRAZZO

Surprised, hah? Ann?

WOODY

Uh . . sure . .

FLESHER

No hard feelin's then . . huh? Cut him a piece of cake. Coconut on th' top . . (*goes to men's room*) Come on out . . What'd you fall in? It's . .

WOODY

(*ahead of Flesher at men's room*) No . . (*to Flesher and Grazzo*) She isn't feeling well. Uh . . look . . I appreciate the party but . . I think I better get her home . . you understand how it is . .

FLESHER

What's th' matter with her? She got th' clap?

GRAZZO

Hey. Did we scare ya?

WOODY

Yeah, yeah . . you did . . Look . . She ate something lousy for dinner . . you know . . I'll take her home. Thanks for the party.

GRAZZO

Sick, huh?

FLESHER

In th' stomach?

WOODY

Right . . yeah, right.

FLESHER

She pregnant?

WOODY

(*nervous*) Ha, ha, ha . .

GRAZZO

How did you like when I moved the puppet around . . How was that?

WOODY

Great . . look . .

FLESHER

We could give you a hand with her.

WOODY

No, I'll handle it . . Look, I could meet you later. Why don't I meet you guys somewhere later . . I'll buy whatever . .

FLESHER

Good idea . .

GRAZZO

We could go over to yer place . . if yer wife's . .

FLESHER

Naw . . Whattaya think, Woody?

WOODY

That's no idea. What about . . Eddie's? I'll buy . . Sure . . sure . . You get over there now . . Get a head start on me . . and . . I'll meet you.

FLESHER

(*goes to the men's room door*) Hope ya feel better . .

GRAZZO

Yeah . .

FLESHER

Hey, Grazzo. You better find a box . . wrap up the cake. An' don't stick yer hand in it this time. (*a door slams upstairs*)

GRAZZO

What's that?

FLESHER

Th' wind . . Maybe it's th' wind.

KIT'S VOICE

You stay here, Joe . . (*loudly*) BUD?

JOE'S VOICE

OK, Mister Mills.

FLESHER

Down here.

KIT'S VOICE

Wait up there, Joe . . I'll take care of it.

JOE'S VOICE

Fine. (*Kit arrives in the basement*)

KIT

Why is it so dark in here? What's . .

FLESHER

Lights don't work . .

KIT

I can see that. What the hell's going on here? What was that about people breaking in? Why did you call me?

FLESHER

Mistake . .

KIT

What? (*Woody stands stiffly near the men's room*) What's the matter with you? You clear your stuff out? (*to Flesher*) What are you wearing there?

FLESHER

Mistake, Mister Mills. Grazzo an' me . . we heard voices down here . . thought it was somebody broke in . . It was only Woody an' his girl friend . . Thought we'd scare crooks, but . . They was only lovin' it up.

WOODY

OK, OK . .

FLESHER

They were doin' a little necking . . ha, ha, ha . .

KIT

I see.

144

WOODY

Look . . (*Kit goes to intercom, pushes button*)

KIT

Joe?

JOE'S VOICE

Yes, Mister Mills.

KIT

Check the circuit breakers . . to the left. You see them?

JOE'S VOICE

Aah, right here . .

KIT

The two blue switches . . Flip them back and forth . .

JOE'S VOICE

Right . . (*the lights click on in the basement*)

KIT

(*looking at the cake*) Who does that belong to?

FLESHER

That's fer Woody . . right? (*Grazzo nods; Kit is confused*)

KIT

I don't like this business here . . (*to Flesher*) You were supposed to be at the meeting.

FLESHER

Yeah.

KIT

What do you mean "yeah"? I told you . .

FLESHER

Well, we passed by this place . . saw th' door open, heard voices . . What th' hell. How did we know they was putting on the late late show . .

KIT

(*to Woody*) Where is Ann?

FLESHER

(*before Woody can speak*) In th' can.

KIT

Get her out of there and let's call it a night. (*Woody remains standing, not moving*) Well?

WOODY

She's sick . . I'll take care of her . . You go ahead, Kit . . I'll . .

KIT

I want to see everybody's out of here. Go in and get her. She's sick, we'll get a cab, take her to the doctor.

145

WOODY

Well, I think she better stay here awhile, Kit. I'll take care of her.

KIT

(*moves toward the bathroom*) Come on . . let's call it a night. (*Woody stops him*) What's the matter, kid?

WOODY

Wait . . uh . . let me. Let me talk to her; see how she is. I'll see how she is. (*exits*)

FLESHER

Maybe we could call Doc Sado down here. He's my wife's doc. I'll call him.

WOODY

(*re-enters from the bathroom*) She'll be fine. She wants to stay for a little while . . she'll be OK . .

FLESHER

Maybe she's allergic to ya, Woody. Ya give her a kiss an' she gets sick . . Ha, ha, ha . .

WOODY

Come on. Cut the gag . . some joke . . (*Kit goes to the men's room door*)

KIT

Ann? You sure you'll be all right . . This is Woody's brother. If you need some help don't be scared . . or embarrassed . . or . .

EVA

(*changing her voice*) No . . no . . I'm fine . . (*Kit sees his wife's bag on the sofa; Woody tries to catch Kit's attention*)

WOODY

Kit, listen . . Kit. (*Kit picks up the bag, looks at it*)

KIT

My God . . my God .

WOODY

Listen, Kit . .

KIT

(*pushes Woody away*) Get away from me. Get away . . (*moves to bathroom door*) Eva. (*a yell*) EVA! (*she enters from bathroom and he grabs her arm*) Come on . . (*pulls her to door*)

EVA

No . .

KIT

Eva.

EVA

I'm going . . This time I'm going for good, Kit. Because . . (*thrusts
ticket at him*)

KIT

Eva . . come on . . let's get back to the apartment . . We'll talk . .
come on . . back to the apartment.

EVA

(*pulling away from him*) Get away. Get your hands off . . I'm not going
back to the damn apartment.

KIT

Everything will be fine . . we'll talk . . I . .

EVA

Told you I'm not staying here. I don't want any more talk from you . .
No more of your lies . .

KIT

Lies . .

EVA

Yes! Everything will be fine . . Like yesterday when you said we were
getting out of this dump. Lies. Well, I want a little action out of you,
honey. You know goddamn well where I'm going to be, but I'll tell you
something flat. I won't stay out on the coast long. Get that? Don't try to
get me on the phone, and no phony letters . . You come and see me.
(*moves to exit*) You come and see me . . then we'll talk . . Good-bye.

KIT

(*following*) Listen . . EVA . . EEEVA. Lies . .

WOODY

(*as Kit stands there*) Kit . .

KIT

That . . that ticket . . My God . . (*turns to Woody*) What the hell
did you say to her? She . . She'd never do that. Everything I've tried to
have . . you kill it for me. It's been just . .

WOODY

Kill . .

KIT

She'd never do that . . run out without . . (*pause; looks at Woody's
case*) You . . you're meeting her. You gonna meet her. (*grabs Woody
by the shirt*) That's the plan, is it?

WOODY

Kit, for Chrissake!

KIT

Few goddamn stories. Lies.

WOODY

What the hell are you talking about? Wake up, will you? I came down here to clean out my locker. Listen, Flesher and Grazzo heard what went on down here. (*to Flesher*) He was only kidding about Eva and me . . that we were . . What d'you think, I got her that ticket? (*Kit moves to exit*) Kit, you see I came down here . . started to pack . . I . . (*He takes Kit's arm. Kit turns, slaps Woody across the face. Woody is stunned. Kit moves away. Woody grabs him, whips him around, speaks kindly, gently.*) My God, what's wrong with you? Flesher and Grazzo heard the whole thing down here. You lied to her, Kit . . That's why she's going away . . (*turns to Flesher*) Come on, tell him what happened down here . .

KIT

(*moving for the door*) Come on . .

WOODY

Easy, Kit . . We're just going to get this . . this business between us finished once and for all. You are not going to dismiss me with some kind of hard-sell crap story . . like . . like yesterday with this . . (*pulls out pink slip*) This . . Like when you threw me out of the house . . when I was sixteen years old . . after an accident . . Those days . . those (*stops in disgust*) Flesher, tell him what went on here.

FLESHER

You talkin' to me?

KIT

Let's go, kid.

FLESHER

Come on. You heard him, killer. Let's get th' show on th' road, sports fans. Move it. (*tries to move Woody, but Woody pins his arm behind his back*)

WOODY

Put your hands on me like that and I'll kill you . . I'll kill you. Joke's over here, pal. Let's hear you talk fast. Give him the straight story what happened in here . .

FLESHER

My . . My arm . . Aaaaaaow.

KIT

Woody. Cut it.

FLESHER
Jesus.

WOODY
Let's hear it. Get it out.

GRAZZO
(*yells*) *OK. OK.* OK . . it was a gag. (*winces*)

WOODY
What about the ticket.

GRAZZO
Yeah . . awright . . yeah . . She pulled it out . . said you thought she was at some movie . . He . . he tried to get her to . . to stick with you . . We was kiddin' about them foolin' around . . Yeah. (*Woody lets Flesher go*) He tried to make her stay, see. Swear to God and hope to die.

FLESHER
So that's what happened. Same like when he fired Harris. She gave him the come-on too . . Come on, Grazzo. Let's get outta this dump. Come on. Let's get outta this bughouse. (*they go out*)

KIT
Woody . . listen . .

WOODY
Oh, how you've shoved the blame off on me. Eva here . . and the accident long ago. You . . How you've pushed it on me. Christ.

KIT
No. You know you've blamed yourself for that . . for years . . you . . ran out of the house . . you . .

WOODY
What the hell if I did. You turned me out completely. You sat around judging me. Why, I saw you . . in my sleep like a big judge. Some big goddamn judge. I came over to . . to work down here like that . . Now . . this is fine, pal. Just fine. Sure I've blamed myself because you passed judgment on me, but that's all over now, Kit. Finished. (*laughs at him*) I don't need you. You don't control me, pal! You're buried down here with your Dorothea this . . Dorothea that . . You'll die down here kidding yourself.

KIT
No. I . . I . . never talk about her . . Eva's important . . Eva's important . . and you . .

149

WOODY

(*quickly*) If she's so goddamn important, then go after her. You've got time. Go on. Go and get her. (*yells*) Move. (*pause*) Look at you.

KIT

(*quietly hysterical, to himself*) Nothing . . nothing wrong in talking of Dorothea . . not a thing. Beautiful . . Absolutely beautiful . . She was so damn beautiful, kid. My God . . so beautiful . . I couldn't help loving her . . Kid, I've been looking for his secret . . for Dad's secret . . It's here. I'm sure of it . . down here . . Sometimes I can sense it . . in the walls . . where he sat. But I've never been able to find out how he approached Dorothea . . (*trailing off*) I have work to do . . here . . things have to be put in order . . (*Kit sits at his desk fumbling through papers in a hysterical and blind manner while Woody watches him. The lights dim out.*)

THE END

LEE H. KALCHEIM

. . . And the Boy Who Came to Leave

. . . And the Boy Who Came to Leave by Lee H. Kalcheim was performed at the Theatre in the Round, Minneapolis, on March 18, 19, 20, 26, 27, 1965. It was directed by Douglas P. Hatfield.

Cast of Characters

PAUL   Richard Anderson
JONATHAN   Steve Benson
PETER   Andy Driscoll
SIDNEY   Joan Plunkett

PLAYWRIGHT'S PREFACE

If I were to design some sort of paradise for playwrights, it would include a huge machine in which the writer would deposit his play as soon as he finished it. The machine would then cast, rehearse, and produce the play immediately. The playwright seeing the production would then rewrite . . and go through this process again, until he was satisfied.

I should think better plays would be written. Plays are difficult to write, because they must really be performed in order for anybody to tell how effective they will be. A good playwright has a theatrical instinct. He is like a computer that changes everything into a code — called a "play" — and it goes down on paper. To be decoded it must be performed. A play is no more a play on paper than a song is a song. You've rarely heard people say, "I read the greatest song the other day." As happy as I am that this play has been published for you to read, I think that reading plays is somewhat silly. You don't get the full effect. You're reading code. Now, think of the playwright who must write the play, and do all the work on it, never really seeing what will work, until it is often too late.

A program like the one the Office for Advanced Drama Research sponsors has come as close to the paradise I described as anything has. The writer lives with his play for weeks, during rehearsals . . works with it while it is on its feet . . tries the changes . . alters it . . and he's no longer in the dark. And then, an audience lets him know where he has gone right — or wrong. Fifteen below zero in Minneapolis may not be paradise weather but it's worth it.

When I brought my play to Minneapolis, it was over three hours long. All the time I'd spent with the script, before coming, I had only cut some three pages. But once rehearsals started, and the play began to breathe, it was easy to cut. You could hear and see the overstatements, the unclear scenes, the inconsistencies in character. Quite a bit was cut. But on opening night, the play still ran three hours plus. The audience handed in critiques, and fortunately the play was done another weekend. In the week between, I cut an epilogue (which does not appear here) and shortened other scenes. The following weekend, it was not only considerably shorter but more dramatically effective. (Not that a good play must be short.) During the run, I had a chance to try different things each night. A chance to experiment. With no pressures. This could never have happened under New York conditions.

I'm hoping, now that these plays are published, that you among the readers who are actively caught up in the theatre, either amateur or professional, will try to put some of them on — and that you who are playgoers only will have the opportunity to see them. Very few people are like Dr. Ballet (2000 new-read plays to his credit) and become adept at anticipating whether a play will work. Nobody really knows until he sees it, so I invite you to be curious enough to produce a new play. Maybe ask the playwright out to see it . . open an office . . get a philanthropic organization behind you . . and . . who knows . .

LEE H. KALCHEIM

New York City
August 1965

THE PLAY

The Scene

An apartment in New York. A large one-room apartment with kitchen area and bathroom off, a bed, a convertible couch, a desk, an old stuffed chair, paintings, a dead plant.

. . . AND THE BOY WHO CAME TO LEAVE

ACT ONE

At rise, Paul sits in the chair with a pad in hand. The phonograph sits on the floor by him. He is listening to a rock and roll record. Other records are scattered about.

SONG

> Ohhhhh I need you and you need me
> That's the way it's got to be . .
> Ohhh ho ho oooooooooo OOOOOOOOO ahhhh
> Ohhhhhhhhhhhh.
>
> Ohhhhh I need you and you need me
> That's the way it's gonna be . .
> Ohhhhh ba ba ba ba ba ba ba ooohhhhhhhhh.

PAUL

(*takes off the needle and sits back*) Andy Randy has another wopper . . ehhhhhhhh. Andy Randy does it again . . with "I Need You and You Need Me" . . ehhh . . A real wopper for the . . ehh . . a real wopper for any bopper in the mood to . . bop? . . hop? A real wopper for any bopper in the mood to hop . . Heh, that's better than the song. Ehhh . . (*writes down what he has just said*) to hop . . ehhh . . Let's see . . (*picks up another record*) The Black Knights sing . . "Baby Don't Go Home" . . (*He puts the record on. There is the usual rhythm intro and the song starts. The apartment door opens and Jonathan enters. He is a bit weary and a bit drunk.*)

JONATHAN

Isn't it great to be home . . (*the song continues*)

SONG

> OH BA OH BA OH BA OH BA OH BA OHHHHHHHH
> Baby don't go home
> I want you right now . .
> Baby don't go home
> I want some lovin'.

PAUL

Hail Caesar . .

JONATHAN

Hey . . Hey, Signore . . Shhhhhhhh. The baby is sleeping.

PAUL

Yeah, wait, it's almost over . .

JONATHAN

Ohhhh . . (*He stumbles across the room and sits on the couch. The number continues and Jonathan begins to wave his finger as if timidly leading the number. His motion gets bigger and bigger until finally he is up on his feet leading the mock orchestra wildly as the number ends.*) Don't . . Go . . Hooooooooooome! (*Jonathan bows*) Now may I remove the needle . .

PAUL

Yes, doctor . . (*Jonathan takes the needle off the record*)

JONATHAN

And what shall we say about this brilliant little piece . . does . . ah . . (*picks up record*) does . . ooops . . *Do* the Black Knights have another smasheroo? . .

PAUL

Don't knock it. I'm doing well tonight. Listen to this for sheer poetry. Andy Randy does it again. A real wopper for any bopper in the mood to hop . .

JONATHAN

Dylan Thomas . .

PAUL

That was "I Need You and You Need Me" . .

JONATHAN

Why don't you just say the same thing for this one . . What is it, "Baby Don't Go Home" is a real . . what was it?

PAUL

Wopper . . Hey, Jonathan.

JONATHAN

Wopper that bops or hops or . .

PAUL

Hey listen . . Do you know what happened to me today?

JONATHAN

I've always wanted to ask you . . Who reads this silly magazine? (*holds it up*) *Music Man* magazine . . pages and pages and pages of highly inspired criticism . . of rock and roll records. Now who cares . . I mean does a record flop if you pan it?

PAUL

Jonathan . .

JONATHAN

"Baby Don't Go Home" is "trash," says Paul Reston of *Music Man* mag . . and then what . . nobody buys it . . how sad . .

PAUL

Jonathan, will you let me tell you the great thing that happened. Do you know what?

JONATHAN

Do *you* know what.

PAUL

Let me tell you . . you see . .

JONATHAN

Let me tell *you* . . Do you know what happened to *me*?

PAUL

No . . Jonathan, what . . you didn't get a job.

JONATHAN

No no no no no no no.

PAUL

You met a friend.

JONATHAN

No, will you shuddup. No, I didn't meet a friend. I met a conspiracy!

PAUL

Oh . .

JONATHAN

I just found out that the whole City of New York is one conspiracy. Every bar in the city is linked by a gigantic system. You see . . you see . . I forgot to pay for a beer at the Avenue bar . . and I couldn't get a drink anywhere . . I'm blacklisted.

PAUL

Well, what happened about the job?

JONATHAN

Nothing happened. They didn't have anything. You know. I think there's something about me. I walk into an office and I sit down . . and they look at me . . and there's something about me that says . . "Don't hire this one. Don't touch him. He's a failure."

PAUL

You haven't been at it long enough. It takes time.

JONATHAN

Ohhh, don't be cute. One minute you tell me I'm just starting . . and then you tell me I'm lazy. Now make up your mind. What am I?

PAUL

You are . . a beer thief . . (*shoots him*) KKKKKkkkkkkkkkkkkkkk.

JONATHAN

That's it . . that's it . . a failure at twenty-eight . . and a beer thief.

PAUL

Look, let me tell you about today. You remember I told you I took the opera down to NBC to show that guy who was interested.

JONATHAN

Your opera. Is that the one that I like?

PAUL

The one that you like . . Anyhow, Jeff and I had a meeting this after-noon with this guy . . Morrison . . and he'd read it, you know . . and we didn't know what to expect . . we'd expected he'd kind of sit and smile . . and thank us . . and that would be all.

JONATHAN

Just like they do to me.

PAUL

So . .

JONATHAN

So . .

PAUL

So . . he sat and smiled . . and he starts coming on with "This is a brilliant little piece" and "How long have you two worked on this to-gether" and "How did you choose opera as your medium, you handle it so well," etc., etc., etc., etc. So'm saying to myself . . OK OK . . now tell us why you can't help us . . Anyhow . .

JONATHAN

Anyhow . .

PAUL

He says . . "I like it . . I'm going to see what I can do. I've passed it

160

on to Ted Brewer, he's head of programming. And I sent a copy over to
Hallmark . . who might be interested. Call me in a couple of days." How
do you like *that*? Can you see that opera on television? Huh?

JONATHAN

And who would watch it?

PAUL

You and me . . and my mother . . who cares? Isn't that great?

JONATHAN

Ha, hah! And then of course. On to the Met.

PAUL

(*sings*) "It's on to the Met. It's on to the Met." I could quit my job . .
How about that!

JONATHAN

And you could recommend *me*. How about that. I'd bring rock and roll
to its knees.

PAUL

Hey. How about that restaurant job you were going to see about. What
happened?

JONATHAN

Nothing. I didn't bother.

PAUL

Why not?

JONATHAN

I'd probably screw something up . . I don't know . .

PAUL

How can you screw up what you haven't tried . .

JONATHAN

I can screw up anything . . tried or untried . . I would turn customers
away . . I would send people fleeting at the door . . I would say . .
How many sir? . . and off they'd go . . No one wants to eat at a restaurant where a failure is host . .

PAUL

You like that word, don't you?

JONATHAN

It's a great word . . Failure . . Fail—ure . . I fail . . You fail . .
We fail . . They fail . . Failure. It's a good word . . Take Success . .
Suc—cess . . That's a terrible word . . How about if Failure meant
when you made it, and Success meant when you failed . . Then . .
maybe Failure wouldn't be an ugly word, huh . . Then everybody would
want to be a failure . . We'd have failure stories . . Lindy Fails to Fly

161

Atlantic . . Hillary Fails to Climb Everest . . Jonathan Dill Fails to
Get Job at Publishing Company . . doesn't sound bad after that, does
it? . . does it? . . Jonathan Dill . . ahhhhh . . It's a conspiracy . .

PAUL

It's your own conspiracy, friend . . You only get up at two in the afternoon because you want to . .

JONATHAN

I didn't say it wasn't my fault. I do not deny fault. I accept it . . I accept my failure. In fact, I rather like it.

PAUL

What now, charity . .

JONATHAN

Ohhhhh. Don't you see. Don't you see . . The conspiracy is against the
ones who succeed. Against you. You see, a failure is pitied . . a success
is envied. How many people are green with envy . . when you say . .
ah . . ah . . Rockefeller, J. Paul Getty, Onassis . . but you mention
a failure . . Give me a failure if you can remember one.

PAUL

Fred Merkle.

JONATHAN

Whoossat?

PAUL

He lost a World Series when he forgot to touch second base.

JONATHAN

What is he? Some kind of a renowned failure?

PAUL

Yeah, some kind of a . .

JONATHAN

Well, doesn't everyone feel sorry for him?

PAUL

I never asked . .

JONATHAN

Don't you feel sorry for him?

PAUL

Ehhhhh.

JONATHAN

Yeah, you feel sorry for him . . He missed the base . . And he lost
the whole shootin' match. I feel sorry for him . . Well, which is better
. . to be envied . . or to be pitied? . . Pity breeds love . . Envy . .

Envy breeds hate . . Therefore my friends . . I . . choose failure . .
(*bows and walks off toward the bathroom*)

PAUL

Jonathan . . you drank all my gin . .

JONATHAN

Eh?

PAUL

You drank all my gin . .

JONATHAN

I know . . I know . . Last night . . I was feeling sorry for myself so
I drank all your gin.

PAUL

Why feel sorry? With all the love you must be getting . .

JONATHAN

I'll buy you another bottle tomorrow . .

PAUL

With what?

JONATHAN

Don't worry about it . .

PAUL

With what?

JONATHAN

With love . . (*exits to bathroom; speaks off*) Heyyyyy, what time is it?

PAUL

About two-thirty . .

JONATHAN

Late . .

PAUL

I guess so . .

JONATHAN

Heyyyyy . . I can't see myself in the mirror . .

PAUL

Turn off the hot water . .

JONATHAN

It's not on . . I just can't see myself . . I think I disappeared . .
Heyyyyy, is that possible . . is it possible to just disappear . .

PAUL

I don't know . . It never happened to me . .

JONATHAN

I think I disappeared . .

PAUL

Turn off the hot water . .

JONATHAN

I told you it's not on . . Heyyyyy, come in here and see if I'm standing in front of the mirror . .

PAUL

You come out here . .

JONATHAN

I think . . (*There is a crash from the bathroom. Paul rushes in. He enters holding Jonathan and carrying him out, takes him to the couch, sits him down.*)

PAUL

You all right?

JONATHAN

Hmmmmm. Yeah . . yeah . . I just got dizzy . . I disappeared. You know that. You got the damndest mirror.

PAUL

You drank too much.

JONATHAN

Oh, I know that. I shouldn't have fallen down . . but the floor slants. I mean the way they keep these buildings up is a sin.

PAUL

It's all right.

JONATHAN

No, it's not all right. Leasing you an apartment with a slanted bathroom is an unpardonable sin. I wonder if disappearing is a sin . .

PAUL

Why don't you go to bed.

JONATHAN

Why don't I . .

PAUL

And pick your things up . . please. I'm tired of tripping over your things . . I damn near killed myself on a pair of your loafers tonight.

JONATHAN

Ooooooooooo. That would be terrible, death by a loafer!

PAUL

I don't care about tripping . . but you leave your underwear around and your shirts and it's just messy. I begin to sound like a mother hen asking you to pick up all the time. That's what I don't like.

JONATHAN

Sounding like a mother hen.

PAUL

That's what I don't like . .

JONATHAN

Well, I will pick up for you then . .

PAUL

That's what you said last week . .

JONATHAN

Tha's a good moral . . (*looking around*) Heyyyyy did you see my filter . . my tar filter . .

PAUL

No.

JONATHAN

Ehhhhh. (*pulls suitcase from under bed, opens it, and fumbles through mess*) I have another one in here somewhere . .

PAUL

I thought you were going to bed . .

JONATHAN

I want a cigarette . . but I need my tar filter . .

PAUL

Why don't you put your stuff in my bottom drawer instead of living out of that suitcase?

JONATHAN

What's the difference . . I'm not going to be here that long . . It's just a visit.

PAUL

Well, you stop that nonsense. I told you you could stay as long as you liked.

JONATHAN

Ah . . here it is . . in my pocket . . (*takes a crumpled cigarette from same pocket, puts it in the filter, and lights it*) Ahhhhh.

PAUL

You can use the bottom drawer.

JONATHAN

I know . . I know . . You're a brick . . a rectangular, red clay, rock and roll brick. But I won't stay too long . . unless I get a job tomorrow . . unless . . I die here . . or disappear here . . or something . . You know what I'd like to do . . I'd like to die and come back as a Tif-

165

fany lantern . . and sit in an antique shop and have old ladies remember me when I was hanging in their parlors. But tonight, I sleep!

PAUL

OK . . OK . . You want some help with the bed . .

JONATHAN

Nooooo. My first success will be the conquest of a Castro Convertible . . Now, ladies and gentleman . . watch this miraculous feat . . Watch as with my bare hands I change an insignificant looking little couch . . into an insignificant looking little bed . . (*takes pillows from couch*) Pillows? . . (*heaves them; Paul picks them up*) Bed . . (*He struggles and finally opens it up. Paul retreats to his chair. Jonathan starts straightening out sheets, etc.*) I thought maybe I'd find somebody in here . . I've always been afraid this thing would close up on me and no one would remember . . and I'd be crumpled up inside pounding at the springs . . whimpering . .

PAUL

You might just sit there and listen . .

JONATHAN

Yes . . wouldn't that be the place . . beneath the boudoir couch he hears a thousand tales of love and intrigue . .

PAUL

You ought to take those sheets to the laundry . .

JONATHAN

Yes . . yes . . tomorrow . . Tomorrow is laundry day and interview day . . a big day is tomorrow . . said Christopher Robin . .

PAUL

. . to Alice . .

JONATHAN

He is making up the bed and singing:

> Jon, Jon the grey ghost is gone
> And the fox is on the town oh . .
> Town oh . . town oh . .
> Jon, Jon the grey ghost is gone
> And it must be a very fine town oh . .
>
> Jon, Jon the grey ghost is gone
> And it must be a very fine town oh.

PAUL

Jonathan . .

JONATHAN

> Town oh . . town oh
> Jon, Jon . . the grey ghost . .

PAUL

Jonathan?

JONATHAN

Ehhh?

PAUL

Please . .

JONATHAN

Ohhhhh sorry . . I didn't think you were working . . (*they continue both working silently for a minute*)

PAUL

It's grey goose . .

JONATHAN

Eh?

PAUL

It's grey goose not grey ghost . .

JONATHAN

What . .

PAUL

Jon, Jon the grey goose is gone . . not ghost . .

JONATHAN

Ohhhhh. Is it . . Sounded like ghost on the jukebox . . (*they continue working*) I like ghost better than goose . . don't you . .

PAUL

Eh?

JONATHAN

Don't you like ghost better than goose . .

PAUL

I never thought about it . .

JONATHAN

Listen:

> Jon, Jon the grey goose is gone
> And it must be a very fine town oh . .

or

> Jon, Jon the grey ghost is gone
> And it must be a very fine town oh . .

Isn't ghost better . .

PAUL

It's goose . .

JONATHAN

Ghost is better . . it sounds like the town really lost something . . Who cares about a grey goose when there's a grey ghost running around . . Jon . . Jon . .

PAUL

Jonathan . . please . .

JONATHAN

Sorry . . (*sits on bed and takes off shoes*) Ohhh . . tomorrow is laundry and interview day . .

PAUL

Did you . . ah . . get your résumé typed up at your friend's office?

JONATHAN

No . . I . . didn't have time . .

PAUL

Didn't have time . . what were you doing?

JONATHAN

I . . met an old friend for lunch . . Sidney . .

PAUL

How long did you have lunch with him?

JONATHAN

It's a her . . Sidney is a girl . .

PAUL

Oh . .

JONATHAN

It's a girl I knew from school . . So we had lunch.

PAUL

You bought her lunch . .

JONATHAN

Ehhh. It was a delightful lunch . . father confessor . . And then we walked in Central Park and watched the old ladies feed the pigeons . .

PAUL

What are you going to do at tomorrow's interview?

JONATHAN

I'm going to put a bag over my head . .

PAUL

Why don't you just wear a nose that lights up . .

JONATHAN

There is an idea . .

PAUL

Jonathan, you *should* have some kind of a résumé.

JONATHAN

Well . . I'll . . Give me some paper . . I'll write one . . (*wanders to desk*) What paper should I take . .

PAUL

Are you going to do it right . .

JONATHAN

I don't know . . I'm going to write a résumé . . so that they can not only look at my face, they can look at my past . .

PAUL

If you're not going to do it right . . just forget it . .

JONATHAN

(*comes back with paper*) Here. Here . . here . . I'll write one out . . (*sits on bed*) Now . . what do I put first . .

PAUL

Who's the interview with?

JONATHAN

I don't remember.

PAUL

Who is the interview with?

JONATHAN

Oh . . well . . it's with a friend of a friend of someone at an art gallery.

PAUL

What gallery?

JONATHAN

Ummmmm . . The Stone Gallery or Shone Gallery or something. It's on Madison Avenue . .

PAUL

Oh . .

JONATHAN

Now let us begin . .

PAUL

In the beginning . . God created Jonathan Dill . .

JONATHAN

That's very good . . Does that come before or after my name . .

PAUL

Here let me have it . . (*takes paper from Jonathan, goes to desk, and puts it in the typewriter*) All right . . Now let's do this thing right . .

JONATHAN

Yes . . I always say . . if you're going to do something . . do it right . . because if you do it wrong . . You get a reputation as someone who always does wrong . .

PAUL

Name?

JONATHAN

You know my name.

PAUL

You don't have a middle name.

JONATHAN

I do, but I don't like it.

PAUL

What is it?

JONATHAN

It's Marshall.

PAUL

What's wrong with that?

JONATHAN

Jonathan Marshall Dill. I don't know . . It sounds like a Kentucky colonel.

PAUL

All right . . Jonathan M. Dill . .

JONATHAN

What's wrong with just Jonathan Dill . . That has a nice ring to it . . I've always wanted to be an executive so that someone could say . . If anyone can do it . . Dill will . . 'Tain't funny McGee . .

PAUL

No . . just Jonathan Dill . .

JONATHAN

Ahh . . Maybe if I changed my name . . it would bring me luck . .

PAUL

How about Bernard Berenson . .

JONATHAN

That's good. I'll use it . .

PAUL

OK. (*types*) I left out the M . . And . . the address. (*types*) . . OK . . ah . . Education?

JONATHAN

Why . . Why can't you just put "yes" down for all those things. Educa-

tion: Yes! Background: Yes. Experience: Yes . . You know . . a very
affirmative résumé . .

PAUL

For a yes-man . .

JONATHAN

For a yes-man . . that's very funny . . for a yes-man . . Ho-Ho. I'm
going to have a drink . . will you join me . .

PAUL

No . .

JONATHAN

You're supposed to say yes.

PAUL

No. (*Jonathan goes to shelves, takes a bottle of Scotch, and pours some
in glass*)

JONATHAN

You sure you don't want some . .

PAUL

No . . Come on, Jonathan, let's finish this so you can go to bed and I
can work . .

JONATHAN

All right . .

PAUL

Education.

JONATHAN

Well, what do I put . . I've been to about twenty different schools . .

PAUL

Well, just your high school . . and where you graduated college . .

JONATHAN

Prep school, one year at military academy . . and then I left there when
I got thrown off a horse and got a brain concussion, which I always tell
my mother is the reason I drink. You see then I can blame her . . because she wanted me to go to the military school . . So I blame her when
I drink . . My mother . .

PAUL

High school . .

JONATHAN

Norman Bleeker High . .

PAUL

Norman Bleeker High?

171

JONATHAN

That's the name of it . . Norman Bleeker was a fireman who gave his life when the old Thomas Jefferson High School burned down . . so they forgot about Thomas Jefferson and they named it after Norman Bleeker . . You know I've told that stupid story a thousand times . .

PAUL

(*types*) College?

JONATHAN

I told you . . I went to one . . two . . ahh . . four different colleges . . Just put the last one . .

PAUL

(*types*) B.A.?

JONATHAN

I don't know . . I guess so . . I never remember getting a degree . .

PAUL

B.A.

JONATHAN

What's the other . .

PAUL

B.S.

JONATHAN

No. I'm B.A. . . Except for da Vinci, I don't understand scientists . . But da Vinci . . was my kind of scientist . . He was a tinkerer . . And I like Galileo . . because he was a martyr . .

PAUL

That's a good reason . .

JONATHAN

It is . . because . . I could never be a martyr . . because I don't care enough about anything yet . . to die for it . .

PAUL

Care about this interview tomorrow . .

JONATHAN

Not enough to die for it . .

PAUL

Just enough to make a good showing . .

JONATHAN

Well, Galileo made a good showing . . and da Vinci made a good showing . . And . . Oops . . I'm putting myself in the company of greatness again . .

PAUL

Maybe . . ah . . if you get used to it . . You'll work toward it . .

JONATHAN

You stink . . Give me a B.A., all right?

PAUL

All right.

JONATHAN

And I thank you. Do you know why I went to three other colleges?

PAUL

You told me . . once, you flunked out of one . .

JONATHAN

I flunked out of one . . and the other two . . I left because I broke out.

PAUL

You broke out? They locked all the students in?

JONATHAN

No no no no no no . . I broke out. I broke out with a rash. It's a rash I get when I have acute discomfort and disenchantment. It's a disease of the young. I haven't had it in a long time. I never got it after my first year in the army. It's like homesickness. Only you don't want to be home. You want to find home . . understand?

PAUL

You found home at the fourth college . .

JONATHAN

And . . in Italy . . in the army . . And when I came back . . I found that . . I could find home . . if I tried a little harder . . So . . I never got a rash at school . . did I?

PAUL

I don't remember . .

JONATHAN

Well, you would have noticed it . . I never got a rash . . there . . So . . if one doesn't come . . here . . soon . . You'd better be careful . .

PAUL

I told you you could stay as long . .

JONATHAN

I know . . I know I know . . I'm just kidding . .

PAUL

All right . . After you graduated . .

JONATHAN

I met Sidney at school . . and she had the same disease . . Only she

173

would cry . . Women cry . . and men love it . . I remember I had
Sidney down for a weekend. One . . night . . we cried together . .
y'know that . . we got so loaded . . we . . cried . . together . . It
was magnificent . . Then we started laughing . . and then I fell down
. . and broke my glasses . . and I took all the glass out . . and we
walked all over campus showing people how she could put her fingers
through my glasses . . I was the magician and she was my helper girl . .
and we both fell down in a hedge by the college chapel . . and . . in
the morning the bells woke us up . . and we went to church . . and no
one would sit next to us because we smelled of liquor . . and . . somewhere . . after that . . I got . . my B.A. degree . .

PAUL

And Sidney . .

JONATHAN

She . . broke out . . she's in town now . . I took her to lunch today . .

PAUL

Today . .

JONATHAN

Yes . . She still breaks out I think . . Yes.

PAUL

(*types*) Uhh . . Experience? What work have you done . . Oh . . Let
me put in your army service . . How long were you in Italy?

JONATHAN

Two years . . Right before school . . (*Paul types*) "I shall return" . .

PAUL

I didn't know we had any troops there . .

JONATHAN

I didn't either . . that's what was great about it . . I worked for the
chaplain . . He didn't know there were any troops there either . .

PAUL

Forget it, tell me all the jobs you've had before . .

JONATHAN

There weren't many . .

PAUL

Tell me them . . even if they were only for a day . .

JONATHAN

Well . . I ah . . ah . . I can't think of anything.

PAUL

You must have done something . .

JONATHAN

Well, I don't know . .

PAUL

Well, somethin' . . Like . . any stupid little thing . . Like once I sold girl scout cookies . .

JONATHAN

You sold girl scout cookies.

PAUL

Yeah, I sold girl scout cookies . .

JONATHAN

The boy scouts don't make cookies, do they . .

PAUL

No . . they tie knots . . and you can't sell knots . .

JONATHAN

No, you can't . .

PAUL

I had a crush on a girl. And she was a girl scout. So I helped her sell girl scout cookies . .

JONATHAN

And did you get the girl . .

PAUL

Ahhhhh . . I think so . . for a month or so . . Then I got tired of her . . and I sold magazines . . Didn't you ever sell . . even magazines?

JONATHAN

Oh! Last summer. I sold encyclopedias . .

PAUL

Good . .

JONATHAN

But that doesn't have anything to do with working in a gallery . .

PAUL

They just want to know first of all whether you're reliable . . They'd like to know if you held other jobs . .

JONATHAN

What's reliability have to do with talent . .

PAUL

Well, let's say they'd rather have a reliable talent than an unreliable talent.

JONATHAN

Hhhh . . maybe Michelangelo was late every day for work at the Sistine Chapel . . So what?

PAUL

Just give me the name of the company you worked for.

JONATHAN

New World Encyclopedias. I was a brilliant salesman.

PAUL

You were?

JONATHAN

You had to be. They had the whole pitch ready . . the minute you signed up . . It was fantastic . . the whole bit down to a science . . and those poor saps bought those books . . they're paying for them now . . and never knew what hit 'em . .

PAUL

And it was you that hit 'em . .

JONATHAN

It was . . do you know . . that we had a prayer meeting before each night's work . .

PAUL

You mean God helped you sell books . .

JONATHAN

No no no . . after our sales meeting . . the leader . . the one who sold most last night . . would stand up . . and to everybody he would say . . Whatta they want??? and we'd scream BOOKS. Then . . Whatta we gonna do tonight??? ROCK 'EM!!! Whatta we here for? MONEY!!! (*Jonathan rises and, screaming "Money," tears through the apartment, then opens the door and exits. He knocks on the door.*)

PAUL

It's open, Jonathan . . (*Jonathan knocks again*) It's . . (*rises, opens door*)

JONATHAN

Oh, hi . . I'm looking for Mr. Reston . . Does he live here?

PAUL

Come on . . (*Jonathan does the whole pitch like a well-oiled machine, quickly, without thought*)

JONATHAN

Oh Mr. Reston . . My name is Jonathan Dill . . I'm doing special work for Great Lakes University. You've been sent some material . .

176

and I've been sent over to have you fill out a brief questionnaire . . You won't mind a question or two would you . .

PAUL

So . .

JONATHAN

So naturally you say no . . and I'm in . . (*enters*) Mrs. Reston in?

PAUL

No . . she's ah . . in Reno . . suing for divorce . .

JONATHAN

Well, would you have her and the kiddies come down . . So they come . . And I say . . I suppose you're wondering what this is all about . . heh, heh, heh. You laugh a little, you know. OK . . Well recently the Great Lakes University has developed a new item, spending several million dollars . . However, this program will not be available to the public for several months . . In other words it's not on sale. My job which is sponsored by a grant of money from the Old Dominion Foundation . . you're familiar with that aren't you, Mr. Reston? Good. Then I ask you a whole list of questions which don't mean anything and finally . . Now the last question is . . Do you, Mr. and Mrs. Reston, do you believe that education is a continuous and lifelong process? Hmmmmm.

PAUL

Ahhhhh.

JONATHAN

Goood. Well you know what . . we're going to do for you. We're going to make you president of your own bank. I toss you a small plastic bank. (*tosses clock or ash tray*) Catch? (*Paul catches*) Then everybody chuckles . .

PAUL

That's in the script.

JONATHAN

Everybody chuckles . . I say, "You ever see one of these things?" Fine. Well, for the price of a daily newspaper . . one nickel, a dime on Sunday, I can place in your home a complete set of The Great Ideas of Western Man. But you don't want a collector coming around every month for ten years to empty the bank. You'll get so accustomed and friendly you'll have to have him for Christmas and Thanksgiving dinner.

PAUL

Wait, Jonathan. I have an idea.

JONATHAN

So we've developed an alternate plan. Pay off in thirty months. You simply drop in a quarter a day . .

PAUL

Jonathan, why don't I sit down and write you a script for your interview tomorrow?

JONATHAN

What?

PAUL

I'm serious. When you have all the lines the determination is dragged along. You're a salesman.

JONATHAN

It wouldn't matter.

PAUL

I could write one with yourself as the chief product. Just memorize it and go in and rock 'em.

JONATHAN

What'll I do . . Rock 'em!

PAUL

Why not . .

JONATHAN

Just . . just finish the résumé.

PAUL

Jonathan . . why not . .

JONATHAN

Just finish it.

PAUL

I'll write you a script. A complete script . . starting with hello, how are you and ending with I'm very happy to be working for you people.

JONATHAN

I'd forget the lines.

PAUL

Jonathan, it's *not* such a crazy idea.

JONATHAN

For me it's a crazy idea . .

PAUL

Jonathan, there are certain things you have to say to these guys . .

JONATHAN

Paul, I told you it never makes any difference.

PAUL

You've got to sling it . . There are lies that work for you . . You've got to sell yourself . . just like those encyclopedias . . why the hell not . .

JONATHAN

I didn't like selling encyclopedias.

PAUL

You don't have to like selling yourself . . but you have to do it for a start . .

JONATHAN

For a start where . .

PAUL

For a start anywhere . .

JONATHAN

I don't like it . . It doesn't matter. It doesn't make any difference . .

PAUL

Stop saying it doesn't make any difference when you know damn well it does . .

JONATHAN

All right it does . . but I can't do it . .

PAUL

All right it does . . and you can do it . . I'll write it for you.

JONATHAN

Paul, it's not funny . . it's not funny.

PAUL

I'm not being funny . . Let's try *something.*

JONATHAN

I've tried everything . .

PAUL

You haven't tried a goddamn thing . .

JONATHAN

It doesn't make any difference.

PAUL

Will you stop saying that!

JONATHAN

I'm saying what's the truth . .

PAUL

The truth is what anybody believes . . The truth is what the loudest guy shouts . . Can't you sell that . . can't you sell something of you . .

JONATHAN

I don't like it . . I don't like it . . I don't like it . . Do I have to have a better reason . .

PAUL

You haven't got any reason . . You're just lazy . . that's the biggest cover-up of all . .

JONATHAN

All right then I'm lazy. I'm lazy. Then that's what I am and I can't be someone I'm not. That's virtuous, isn't it . . being what you are.

PAUL

Jonathan, stop talking college jargon. It's a big world . . nobody believes that horseshit . . You're living in a big world . .

JONATHAN

It doesn't matter . . People are people . .

PAUL

People are people . . that doesn't mean anything . . that's goddamn jargon . . Jonathan . . You wouldn't know virtue if you tripped over it . . Why don't you just get the opening prayer over with and run out and rock 'em . . just once . .

JONATHAN

All right, forget it . .

PAUL

Just once, Jonathan . .

JONATHAN

Forget the résumé. Forget it . .

PAUL

Let's not forget it . . let's deal with it . .

JONATHAN

I don't care . .

PAUL

Let's deal with it . .

JONATHAN

Paul, I don't care . . You know that . . You know that . .

PAUL

That's a poor excuse . . Let's deal with it . . Let's rock 'em . .

JONATHAN

I'm not rocking anybody . . And don't say that . . it makes me sick . .

PAUL

Rock 'em . . rock 'em rock 'em rock 'em . . rock 'em . . rock 'em . . rock 'em . .

JONATHAN

PAUL I DON'T LIKE THAT! (*they stand silent*) Please . . (*knock on door*)

PAUL

Who is that . .

JONATHAN

It's the Great Ideas salesman.

PAUL

(*goes to door*) Yeah?

PETER

(*from outside*) It's Peter . . (*Paul opens the door and Peter enters*) Hello, screwhead, how are you . . I saw your light on . .

PAUL

It's about three o'clock . .

PETER

You going to bed.

PAUL

Just Jonathan . .

PETER

I'll just stay a minute . . I saw your light . . Get a job . . Jonathan old screwhead . .

JONATHAN

Don't taunt me . .

PETER

You shit . . Listen . . I met this guy today whose father is president of a TV station . . Maybe can get you a job . .

PAUL

Doing what . .

PETER

I don't know . . He said maybe he'd get a job for me . .

PAUL

What do you need a job for . .

PETER

Ehhh . . I get tired of working for my old man . .

PAUL

What's the difference . . for a few months . .

PETER

I may not go back to school . .

PAUL

Who's making the decision . . you or they . .

PETER

I am . . Hell, the dean doesn't give a rusty screw whether I come back or not . . He likes my old man's money . . (*walks over to bed*) How are you, Jonathan . . You still mooching off our friend . .

JONATHAN

I'm not staying much longer . . I have an interview tomorrow . .

PAUL

What do you call what *you* do when you use the phone?

PETER

Hell, I won't use your phone if you don't want me to . .

PAUL

I really don't care . . You can sleep here too if you want . . As long as you don't slobber on the rug . .

PETER

I like you, Paulsie baby . . 'cause you sound like a mean bastard and I know you're just a screwoff . . Let me use your phone.

PAUL

Who are you calling now . .

PETER

I got this chick who's been bugging my ass. I met her last night at a party . . and I've been trying to get her all day and her old lady keeps saying she's out. Well, she won't be out now . .

PAUL

She'll love you if you ever get through to her . .

PETER

She loves my ass . . She told me that last night . .

PAUL

She's eloquent . .

PETER

She was hanging all over me . . I'm telling you . .

PAUL

I know . . I know . .

PETER

But I didn't score 'cause her old man came in on us when I had her on the couch . . I like the guy though . . He's a hot shit . . She went to bed . . and we stayed up and talked for about an hour . . He likes me too . . Yes yes yes . . ahhhhhh. (*looks through address book, dials*) Ohhhh someone's gonna be angry . . Ahhh . . Hello . . Ah . . Robin . . Robin? This is Peter . . Hell, it's three o'clock or something . . I told you I'd call until I got in touch with you . . What are you mad at,

you know you wanted me to call . . Come off it . . Don't look . .
Your old man and I talked for two hours . . He loves my ass . . Hey
. . Look . . How about if I come over . . I'm not going to hang up . .
Come on . . I'll meet you in half an hour . . What's the matter with
you . . what difference does it make . . Look . . Look . . Look . .
you're attracted to me, right . . Tell me . . Look, I'm a good-looking
guy, right . . And you're attracted to me, right . . So why screw
around . . I'll just be there in half an hour . . Robin, what difference
does the time make . . I can't . . I can't . . your mother won't let
me talk to you. I . . Where . . Where's that . . You gonna take me
to dinner? Very funny . . OK . . four o'clock . . five o'clock . .
What time are you through work . . I'll meet you at five right there . .
Don't screw me up now . . You know . . Hey . . come on . . I want
to come over and see if you really have nice legs . . Oh screw that . .
Don't play it . . you don't care what I say . . You've got a nice body,
why play the role about it . . You are . . Look, you're great when
you're drunk . . why did you sober up . . I'm not . . I haven't had
a thing . . I'm in a friend's apartment . . Ahhh . . No party. We're
just talking . . Look . . forget it, Robin . . I'll see you tomorrow
. . Robin Red Breast . . Don't "stop Peter" me . . I called you that
last night and you laughed so hard beer come out of your nose . . Yeah
. . Go to bed, you're terrible . . Go to bed . . I'll see you tomorrow
. . G'night . . Robin Red Breast . . 'Night. (*hangs up*) Screw . .
well . .

PAUL

Pity . .

PETER

You should see this body . .

PAUL

Bring her over some night, we'll all stand around and look at her . .

PETER

Maybe she has a friend . . She is nice . . I don't know if she goes
down though.

PAUL

Well if you don't know . . I don't guess anybody does . .

PETER

She's a little wicked when she's sober . .

PAUL

Aren't we all . .

183

JONATHAN

Here, here . .

PETER

Hey, Jonathan . . You're gonna come with me this weekend . .

JONATHAN

What . .

PETER

I'm going up to school . . for initiation and the party . . Didn't you get the invitation?

JONATHAN

Ohhhh, I don't know . . maybe I did . . I don't know . . look over there.

PETER

Where is this thing, Jonathan . . (*looks for invitation*)

JONATHAN

I don't know . . find it tomorrow . .

PETER

You want to go to bed?

JONATHAN

I've got to get up early . .

PETER

Oh . . you've got an interview . . Well, look, I'm leaving tomorrow afternoon at . . Oh . . shit . . I just told Robin Red Breast I'd meet her at five tomorrow . . I'm going up to school at three . . Eh . . She'll love me more . . Oh . . here it is . . You didn't even open it . . You didn't open it . .

JONATHAN

I know . . I . . didn't . . open it . .

PAUL

We never open mail from school . . They only want money . .

PETER

So send 'em money . . aren't you a loyal alumnus . .

PAUL

Yeah. But I can't afford to be as loyal as they'd like me to be . .

PETER

Here . . (*throws it on the bed*) There it is.

PAUL

(*picks up invitation*) Let me see . .

PETER

It's going to be a great weekend . .

PAUL

"Omega chapter of Sigma Delta Phi requests the pleasure of your company for dinner following the initiation of neophytes. 12 Bushwell Drive, Saturday, Dec. 12, at half after five o'clock. RSVP. Black tie." Shall I read the list of neophytes . . This year's neophytes . . in the purple trunks . . weighing one hundred and seventy pounds . . from Gross Pointe, Michigan . . Weldon P. Weldon . . Hurrahhhhh . . followed by . .

PETER

Come on, Jonathan, it's going to be a blast.

PAUL

After the neophytes comes the blast . . Don't you have to rent a black robe too?

PETER

We don't wear robes . . screwhead . . only the brothers . .

PAUL

Are you a brother . .

PETER

Jonathan and I are brothers . . but not active . . Weren't you ever in a fraternity . .

PAUL

Nope . . I was ugly my freshman year and nobody wanted me . . and by my senior year when they wanted me, I thought they were ugly . . and I didn't want them . . Say . . Why not make me an honorary brother . . Then I can get official invitations . . and sing spook songs . . Here . . (*grabs cover off his bed and throws it over Peter*) One for you . . (*takes blanket*) One for me . . OK . . Now what do I do . . Jonathan . . What do we do now. I know. We recite the great frat pledge and sing the great frat spook song. I, Paul V. Reston III do solemnly swear to uphold the standards of the Sigma Delta Phi Fraternity. And hold the bonds of brotherhood and goodly fellowship of all men of my clan. And . . oh . . of all men of my clan . . above that of all men of any other clan . . And I do swear to protect this great bond of brotherhood in the difficult times of war . . in the dangerous times of tension and in times of peace. For first, last, and always . . Brotherhood must stand above everything . . and if by chance I meet a man and he be black or he be not of Christian faith . . I say to him . . You'll have to find your brotherhood elsewhere . . because here . . we are of the finest crop . . and we must never bend below it . . Our robes are blackest black . . our faces are whitest white . . Our true is the blues true . . and therefore let us rise and sing our . . fraternity song . .

> I need you and you need me
> Sigma Delta Ph-i-i-i
> That's the way it's gonna be
> Sigma Delta Phi-i-i-i
> Ohhhhhh . . Oh Oh Oh . . Oh oh Ohhhhhh

(*parades around, then suddenly flings off blanket and stops*) Well . . am I a brother . .

PETER

If Bob Warfield saw this he'd shit . .

PAUL

Am I a brother?

PETER

Huh, Jonathan . . Wouldn't he . . wouldn't he . .

PAUL

HEY . . AM I A BROTHER?

PETER

What are you screamin' for . .

PAUL

Because you don't listen . . I asked if now I am a brother . .

PETER

Christ, be brother, you're a brother . .

PAUL

OK . . Shake my hand . .

PETER

What are you, off your nut . .

PAUL

No . . I'm not off anything . . I'm just showing the folks back home in television land how great it is to be present at the swearing in of the neophytes . . (*shakes Peter's hand, then Jonathan's*) Thank you . . thank you . . I feel so much better . . (*goes back to the desk*)

PETER

He been drinking?

JONATHAN

Nooo . . he's . . You know . . I . . he gets bugged when he has to listen to those records . . I don't know . .

PETER

Well, are you coming?

JONATHAN

When . .

PETER

Tomorrow at three . . I'm driving up . . There's going to be a party Saturday . . probably one tomorrow too . .

JONATHAN

I got an interview . .

PETER

After that . .

JONATHAN

How about if they hire me . .

PETER

Come on, Jonathan . .

JONATHAN

How about if they hire me . .

PETER

How about that . .

JONATHAN

I don't know . .

PETER

Do you want to come . .

PAUL

Hey, brother . . They might hire him! (*There is a silence as Peter looks at Paul . . rises . . walks away . . picks up a magazine and starts thumbing through it. Jonathan looks, then gets up and goes to the shelf.*)

JONATHAN

Drink . . Peter . .

PETER

No.

JONATHAN

(*takes the bottle, finds a glass, pours a drink, then starts off to bathroom, stops, goes to bureau*) Need a pill . . Need a pill . . (*goes off to bathroom, stops again, picks up a magazine*) Need a magazine . . need a magazine . . (*goes off again; stops*) You both give me the runs . . (*exits in bathroom and closes door; Peter puts down the magazine*)

PETER

Hey . . why don't you do something with him . . (*Paul does not respond*) Hey, shithead . .

PAUL

Can't you go five minutes without using your filthy mouth . .

187

PETER

What is bugging you? Christ, you want me to leave . .

PAUL

I . . forget it . . forget it . .

PETER

I just asked why you don't do something for him . .

PAUL

You didn't just ask that . . You come up here and you slobber all over the rug and you act like a two-year-old Peter . . You've got enough steam inside you to do something constructive . . why drag him off to a college weekend . .

PETER

You didn't answer me, screwhead . . Paulsie . . Paul . . You want him here forever?

PAUL

I really don't care . . He'll stay here as long as he can. I really don't care.

PETER

He's a smart boy . . Why don't you help him out?

PAUL

Oh come on, Peter, he's had too much help. That's his problem.

PETER

Well . . if . . he . . I would help him along. I don't know. He . . respects you. Jonathan told me he thought you had direction. He likes that.

PAUL

He likes anything he doesn't have.

PETER

Come on . .

PAUL

You have direction, don't you?

PETER

I don't have anything. I have balls, that's what I have . . and Jonathan doesn't care about that. He never touched a woman in his life.

PAUL

How do you know?

PETER

You know what I mean by touch.

PAUL

And I say how do you know.

PETER

I don't . . I just . .

PAUL

You just don't . . and it doesn't matter anyway. It hasn't done much for you . . or me, I guess.

PETER

Yeah? You see Robin Red Breast. She'll do something for you.

PAUL

Tell her to get Jonathan a job . .

PETER

She's a job. She's a job.

PAUL

What do you want me to do? Cut his grapefruit up in sections every morning? How *do* you help him? He's drifted around and around and he's got to stop.

PETER

So why does he have to stop *here*?

PAUL

He's got to stop somewhere.

PETER

But why here, Paulsie boy?

PAUL

Well, what do you want me to do? Kick him down the stairs?

PETER

Yes. If you can't help him . . Kick him down the stairs. You don't need him.

PAUL

I'm trying to help him for Christ's sake. You don't kick your friends down the stairs.

PETER

Why not . .

PAUL

Oh you would. You would do just that . . and smile doing it . . And once outside, you'd join Jonathan at the nearest bar.

PETER

So what.

PAUL

So it doesn't get him a job.

PETER

Well, maybe nothing gets him a job, Paulsie boy, maybe nothing.

PAUL

Yeah, that's the answer . . that's the answer. Look. Look. He's got an interview tomorrow morning with some art gallery. So there.

PETER

Jonathan's got an interview with an art gallery?

PAUL

Yeah, some Stone, Shone gallery. Now what am I going to do, *take* him there?

PETER

He's not going to get that job tomorrow.

PAUL

Probably not.

PETER

Not probably not . . definitely not. Definitely not.

PAUL

He might fool us this time. He just might fool us.

PETER

Fool who . . fool who, Paulsie boy. Jonathan already went to that interview. Last week he went to that interview. We met some girl at a party. Nancy Stone. Her aunt runs the place and Jonathan had a lovely chat with that lady . . and that lady told Jonathan she needs help in her two-by-four gallery like a hole in the head. He flunked that interview last week. He didn't tell you?

PAUL

No.

PETER

And you thought . . (*laughs*) Well, he's honest, right? He could have made up an appointment with anybody, but he picked a real place and a real appointment. Maybe he forgot he already went there . .

PAUL

I don't think he forgot.

PETER

Neither do I . .

PAUL

Shhhhh-it.

PETER

Hmmm. Didn't hear you. (*Bathroom door opens, Jonathan teeters out merrily and crosses to bed. Drops magazine.*)

JONATHAN

(*imitating a withered old man*) Rags . . shoelaces . . potholders . .
Rags, shoelaces . . Potholders . . (*sits; a silence*)

PETER

I'll . . ah . . I'll see you . . I'd better shove . . You want to come
with me . .

JONATHAN

Well, let's see how I feel tomorrow. Tomorrow they may crown me king!

PETER

Ah . . I'm leaving . . my place at three . . you . . meet me there
. . You can rent a tux up at school . . R.J. said we could stay in his
room if there's no room at the house. He said they'd be tapping a keg on
Friday . . Maybe Sidney will come along. She . . said she might . .
Hey . . Jonathan . . Hey . . You have to be there . . Don't you
remember? You are the official keg tapper . . You have to perform the
ceremony . .

JONATHAN

Oh . .

PETER

Hey . . screwhead . . You still have that poem . . You know that
thing you read . . You know it . . and that thing . . that highland
fling you did.

JONATHAN

Yeah . . yeah . .

PETER

You have to be there . .

JONATHAN

Ahh . . that's . . Yeah . . The Highland Fling . .

PETER

You have to lead us . . screwhead . . (*sings*)
        Ah . .
        Glorious, victorious. One Keg of Beer for
        The Four of Us.
        Glory be the day, when the Sigmas pass away
        And then, then they'll be no more of us . .
Wait, wait, wait . . (*goes to Jonathan; stands him up*) OK . . ready . .
(*puts an arm around him*)
        Glorious, victorious. One Keg of Beer for
        The four of us

BOTH

Glory be the day, when the Sigmas pass away . .

JONATHAN

And then there'll be . . no more of us . .

PETER

Yeahhhhhhhh ah. OK. Here we go . . (*holds his nose and imitates bag-pipes playing fling*)

Yeahh dad . . ddidddddddd . .

(*Jonathan watches amused; then caught in the stupor of his drink begins a clumsy fling*) Yeah . . yeah . .

PAUL

Peter, there's . . someone . . beneath us . .

PETER

(*continues*) ddd . . dddd . . (*Suddenly Jonathan falls. Paul goes over and the two of them pick him up, one holding each arm.*)

JONATHAN

He is risen . .

PAUL

You all right?

JONATHAN

I flung my highland too far . .

PETER

You OK?

PAUL

Go home . . I'll put him to bed . .

PETER

Why not let him put himself to bed . .

PAUL

Peter . . Go home before I call up Robin Red Breast . . and tell her you're not going to show tomorrow . .

PETER

OK . . Jonathan . . I'll see you at three . . I'll, ah . . I'll call if you're late . . OK? . . OK?

JONATHAN

Yeah . . I'll . . three . . OK . . Good night, Peter . .

PETER

'Night . . (*exits*)

JONATHAN

I'm . . all right . . It's . . the anemia . . It's . . it's not the booze . .

PAUL

Did you take the pill . .

JONATHAN

No . . it . . ah . . fell in the sink . .

PAUL

Here . . (*takes another pill, gets a glass of water, and brings it to him*)
Here . .

JONATHAN

Thank you . . You're a brick . . still . . same brick . . ahhh . .
Thank you . . Ahhh . . Peter's strange, isn't he . . He . . ah . . He
gets on your nerves . .

PAUL

Sometimes . .

JONATHAN

He gets on my nerves . . Lucky . . Peter . . he . . ah . . has no nerves
for people to get on . . Does he . .

PAUL

I don't know . .

JONATHAN

Well, we haven't found any, have we . . Well . . he's all right . . His
intentions are always good . . I mean his long-run intentions . . I
mean . . He just wants to have a good time . . and . . he forgets . .
about important things sometimes . .

PAUL

Ah . . What time are you getting up . . I'll set the clock after I leave.

JONATHAN

Wake me . . with you . . that's good enough. We'll . . get up together.

PAUL

Are you . . ah . . going up to school . .

JONATHAN

Oh . . ah . . I don't know . . Maybe . . Maybe I'd better after my
interview.

PAUL

Yeah . .

JONATHAN

They sort of expect me . . You know I was an officer in the fraternity
. . I was corresponding secretary once . . and pledgemaster once.
So . . I . . should . . go up . . It's a big weekend. Maybe Sidney
will go . .

PAUL

OK . . I'll wake you . .

JONATHAN

OK . . Oh . . wait . . before . . I . . Here . . I have something for you . . I brought a present for you and I never gave it to you . . Where's my overcoat.

PAUL

On the chair . .

JONATHAN

(*rises, picks up coat, goes in pocket, brings out flat little bag*) Here . . Here . . (*draws a record out of it*) Look . . Look it's a record . .

PAUL

I see that . . what is it . .

JONATHAN

Don't . . don't . . don't look . . Just put it on . . Here let me. (*takes the record, goes to machine, and puts it on*) I bought it as a special present for you. I went into this arcade . . Times Square today, you know, where you can get newspapers printed that say "Joe Brody Holds Wildest Party in Town." Well . . I got this . . For you . . Remember this is ever and ever . . Your presente . . signore . . (*puts needle on, sits*)

JONATHAN'S VOICE

This is a recording . . The following will be one minute of absolute silence . . (*they both sit, for one minute, until the click, click of the end of the record*)

PAUL

Turn it off . .

JONATHAN

Oh . . (*does so*) Do . . you like it . . (*begins getting into bed*)

PAUL

(*smiles*) Yes . . It's just what I always wanted.

JONATHAN

You see . . if you play it at least once for every guest . . you'll have your share of peace during the course of the year.

PAUL

Thank you, Jonathan . . I'll mention you in *Music Man* magazine . . as an up-and-coming recording artist . .

JONATHAN

That would be so kind . . At last . . Just to be . . up and coming . . (*slides down in bed*)

Jon Jon the grey ghost is gone
And it must be a very fine town oh . .
Town oh . . town oh . .

Good night . . Paul . . (*pulls out light*)

PAUL

'Night . . (*light at his desk remains*)

JONATHAN

Paul . .

PAUL

Hmmm . .

JONATHAN

Y'know . . I've been thinking . . Whenever I have an interview with someone . . and they're really not interested in what I'm saying . . they disappear . . Does that ever happen to you?

PAUL

I . . don't know . .

JONATHAN

I'm talking . . and I look at them . . and there's this blank expression . . and they're . . somewhere else . . They're home opening their refrigerator or something . . They just disappear . .

PAUL

Uh hum . .

JONATHAN

I wonder . . if . . I wonder if disappearing is a sin. I wonder if disappearing is a sin. I didn't have the hot water on before, Paul, you know that . . I didn't have the hot water on . . I disappeared . . I disappeared . . (*slow curtain as he continues*)

ACT TWO

Scene I

The apartment, the following week. The door opens and Sidney and Jonathan enter. As they enter, they must step over some clothing which is lying in the hall. Jonathan just steps over it and continues in, but Sidney stops.

JONATHAN

Here we are . . The Grand Palace of Monaco . . The Duomo . . the ah . .

SIDNEY

Jonathan . . what's all this . .

JONATHAN

Eh?

SIDNEY

(*picks up some of the things*) Some clothing here in the hall . .

JONATHAN

Oh . . (*returns to pick it up*) Just some of my things . .

SIDNEY

What are they doing out here . .

JONATHAN

Nothing . . nothing . . just . . dirty things . .

SIDNEY

You leave them in the hall?

JONATHAN

No it's a . . it's a . . joke . . it's Paul's joke . .

SIDNEY

Ohh . .

JONATHAN

Here . . give me . . I'll put it away. (*gets the clothes from Sidney, walks with the armful of clothing to the closet which he manages to open, and then simply throws all the clothing in and shuts the door*) Now . . my dear . . will you have a drink . . a drink.

SIDNEY

Ehh . . I don't know . .

JONATHAN

What will you have . .

SIDNEY

I don't know. What are you going to have . .

JONATHAN

Well, we have . . Ah . . You'd better have Scotch . . that's all he has left . .

SIDNEY

All right . .

JONATHAN

(*goes to the refrigerator, pulls out ice cubes and with difficulty knocks out some cubes, leaves the tray out, puts ice in glasses, goes to the bar, pours drinks*) You will have some dinner with me . . All right . . I'm sure there's something hanging around in that big icebox that we can have . . We can always have spaghetti . . do you like spaghetti . .

SIDNEY

I don't care . .

JONATHAN

Good. We can always have spaghetti . . Here . .

SIDNEY

Thanks . .

JONATHAN

So . . We are now in the same fraternity . . The great unwashed un-
employed . . We'll have to celebrate . .

SIDNEY

It's nothing to celebrate . .

JONATHAN

Ohh I think it is . . Sidney, my dear . . you and I are one of the few
uncompromising people left on earth . . Think of all the things we
could be doing . . to just exist . . but we would rather do nothing than
do something that is less than what we would rather do . . *cappiche?*

SIDNEY

No . .

JONATHAN

Yes, you do . . You quit your job today . . and I . . I have such a
condescending nature about me when I look for a job that I don't really
want . . that I don't get it . . So we are both stark raving idealists . .
who at the moment are doing stark raving nothing . .

SIDNEY

But . . I'm going to need some money pretty soon.

JONATHAN

You see you're . . you're not with it . . If you worry you're not with
it . .

SIDNEY

I didn't like making phone calls, but it was money . .

JONATHAN

Well . . together we will keep warm . .

SIDNEY

With what . .

JONATHAN

With . . our convictions . . I wouldn't sit in a little cubicle for thirty-
five dollars a week and say . . "We'd like to tell you that you are for-
tunate enough to be chosen to receive ten free dance lessons as a trial
offer from the Jay Studios. Isn't that wonderful? Wouldn't you like to
begin immediately?" The hell with them . .

SIDNEY

But I've got to make something . .

JONATHAN

I'll take care of that . . we'll put you where you belong . . You know
. . Peter . . Peter knows a lot of people . . he'll get you a job. .

SIDNEY

Why didn't he get you one . .

JONATHAN

He doesn't know that kind of people . .

SIDNEY

What kind does he know . . If they're like his friends . .

JONATHAN

No . . but he could get you a job . . as a . . a . . what do you want
to do?

SIDNEY

I don't know . . I don't want to work really . . I want to go back to
school . .

JONATHAN

Well, you see . . you shouldn't have left . .

SIDNEY

I didn't have any choice . .

JONATHAN

Ohhhhh, I suppose when you come down with rheumatic fever . . you
don't have any choice . . but I don't see why you didn't go back . .

SIDNEY

I wanted to go back . .

JONATHAN

And . .

SIDNEY

My parents . . wanted me to . . ah . . stay home for a year . . They
. . they . . think I only got sick because I didn't take care of myself . .
and they wanted me to stay home . . and get a job . . so they could
watch me . .

JONATHAN

Watch you what?

SIDNEY

I don't know . .

JONATHAN

What are they going to watch . . It seems to me they'll just stand around and watch out for little viruses . . to make sure they don't attack you . . that's what it seems to me . .

SIDNEY

Oh . . it's much more than that . . They . . want me home . . They want me to go to school in the city . . My mother was going to get me a job with her at the Red Cross . . and I said no . . So my father told me that I'd have to go out and work for myself . . They wouldn't buy any clothes for me or pay for anything except bed and board . . He got on this real jag . . So . . I don't know . . I'd like to move out . .

JONATHAN

Don't they want you to go to school . . and get your very important degree . .

SIDNEY

They want me to be something like a wife . . or . . they think I'm irresponsible . . They think I got sick because I didn't take care of myself . . I'm supposed to be home every night before eleven . .

JONATHAN

Are you going to school next year . .

SIDNEY

If I'm a good girl . . If I keep a steady job and get eight hours' sleep.

JONATHAN

They know you quit?

SIDNEY

No. They . . don't know . . I had a job before this I quit too. They still think I'm working at the public library . . I didn't like that either . . filing books . .

JONATHAN

Don't they check . .

SIDNEY

I don't know . . They don't care . . I just tell them I'm there . . They don't check . . they don't care . . As long as I come home on time . . and drink juice . . As long as I have enough money to buy what I need . .

JONATHAN

Well that's not much . .

SIDNEY

I'm going to get an apartment . . and stay there as much as I can . .

JONATHAN

That would be lovely . . we could go in on that together . . You could

199

stay there days . . and I could stay there nights . . And weekends we could go away . . You're allowed away on weekends . .

SIDNEY

If . . they know where I'm going . . Peter gives them a line about taking care of me and they fall for that . . That's how I went up to school . .

JONATHAN

I'll work days . . and you'll live there . . and . . No better yet . . I'll work nights . . and we'll spend our days together . . How about, my dear . . if we get secretly married . . how about that . .

SIDNEY

That's all I need . .

JONATHAN

Well, I think that is a grand idea . . I think we should get married . .

SIDNEY

Jonathan . . (*touches his cheek*)

JONATHAN

Let me get you another drink, my dear . .

SIDNEY

I'm all right . .

JONATHAN

Jack . . (*rises and goes to bar and pours drink, goes to get ice, opens refrigerator, then sees cubes on the table*) Ooops we're melting . . (*takes a wet cube and drops it in, returns to Sidney*) I think that's a wonderful idea . . a place of our own . . And I could sit and write my poems . . and you could do whatever you want . . You could . . We could teach each other. What's a college professor anyhow . . just a man who keeps a chapter ahead of his students . . So I'll keep a chapter ahead of you on one subject . . and you on another . . and we'll lecture each other . . every day . . every day . .

SIDNEY

How will we live . .

JONATHAN

I told you I would work at night . .

SIDNEY

What would you do . .

JONATHAN

I would . . I would simply open my doors to contributions. I would hold sessions. Yes. Yes . . Sessions. Anyone who wanted to come and talk to me could come and talk. And we would invent a language of our

own . . you see . . We would not talk in conventional languages . .
We would just talk in no language . . but we would express ourselves
. . Like . . I would say to you . . zaba zaaba . . deeee deeee ooh
. . See? Now what have I said . .

SIDNEY

I don't know . .

JONATHAN

Well . . just answer me then . . zaba aba dee dee ohh . .

SIDNEY

(*laughs*) What do I say . .

JONATHAN

No no no no . . don't react . . just say the first thing that comes to
your mind . .

SIDNEY

Like what . .

JONATHAN

Like if I say . . zaba dee dee ohh . . you say . . Owa waaaa. It's not
what you say . . it's how you say it . . See . . it's like . . Take my
hand . . (*she does*) Now . . when I squeeze . . you squeeze back ac-
cordingly . . OK . . (*he squeezes; they exchange a few squeezes*)
That's wonderful . . but you don't have to squeeze hard if I squeeze
hard . . you can change . . you can change . .

SIDNEY

What's the . . sense . .

JONATHAN

There's no sense . . except . . we've got to pay so much attention to
what we're doing . . that we make contact . . and that is very important . . Here . . answer me . . Zoolo . . gagba weeegeee . . (*Sidney laughs*) Go ahead . . say anything . . just make a noise . .

SIDNEY

No . . it's silly . .

JONATHAN

You're thinking too much . .

SIDNEY

I can't do it . .

JONATHAN

Oh you can . . you can . . just . . use the alphabet . . I'll say letters
and you say letters . . OK . . ahh . . A Z B D F? Say some letters.

SIDNEY

Ahhhhh, Q R S T . .

JONATHAN

Listen to me . . B R D T Y . . R?

SIDNEY

L B D N Y . . (*laughs*)

JONATHAN

(*jumps up and screams*) N U F T L Y D . . B? (*points to her*)

SIDNEY

(*reacts immediately*) Ahhh, C . . D . .

JONATHAN

Marvelous . . You just . . (*genuinely excited over his discovery*) you . . just had the most wonderful bewildered look on your face when I screamed at you . . and you just said two letters of the alphabet. It was marvelous . .

SIDNEY

What . . good is it, Jonathan . .

JONATHAN

It's good for us . . It gives us a whole new dimension . . Why my dear it may even replace sex as a sensual activity . . The alphabet in all its glory . .

SIDNEY

Jonathan . . sit down a minute . .

JONATHAN

My dear . . it's time to make some supper . .

SIDNEY

I'll help you . .

JONATHAN

All right . . come . . let's see what there is to make . . (*they hold hands and troop off to the kitchen area*) Ahhh. Here's some spaghetti . . and what's this . . apple sauce . . Hmmm . . Soup . . hmmm. Let's see about the refrigerator. (*opens refrigerator*) Ehhh . . Oohhhhh here's something . . (*opens tinfoil*) Some sausages . . I love sausages . . Good Italian sausages . . (*smells*) I think they're good . . smell . . (*she does*)

SIDNEY

I don't know . .

JONATHAN

All right . . we'll have sausages and spaghetti . . You put water in a pan . . and I'll cook the sausages . .

SIDNEY

What pan . .

JONATHAN

Take that one there . . just fill it with water and put it in . . I'll do this
. . (*Jonathan takes a frying pan that is hanging and proceeds to put
sausages in it while Sidney fills the pot with water*)

SIDNEY

Now what . .

JONATHAN

Put it on the stove . . there . . Now . . I'll light this . . (*turns on
stove*) There . . NOW all we do is wait . .

SIDNEY

You sure . .

JONATHAN

Sure . . you just . . Oh . . Put the spaghetti in . .

SIDNEY

Now?

JONATHAN

I guess so . . Just put it in till it's soft . . Here . . (*dumps whole box
in*)

SIDNEY

That's a lot . .

JONATHAN

We'll eat a lot . . it shrinks . . I think . . All right . . we'll be ready
in no time . . We'll be . . hummmmm (*goes to bar to get another
drink, pours more in glass*) Do you want some more . .

SIDNEY

A little. (*Jonathan gives her more*) Your ice is all melted . .

JONATHAN

Ohhhhh. Here, have some cold water . . (*pours cold water from tray in
each drink, then puts tray back in refrigerator*) OK . . now I must read
you the poem that I wrote today in the subway . . Come and sit . .

SIDNEY

Ah . . all right . . Ah . . Jonathan . . the sausage is smoking . .

JONATHAN

Ohhh . . that's all right . . that's supposed to . . Ehhh, come sit . .

SIDNEY

That much . .

JONATHAN

Yes . . yes . . come sit . . it's smoked sausage . . it's supposed to
smoke . . (*they go back and sit down*) Now . . now . . listen . .

(*reaches in his pocket and pulls out a crumpled piece of paper*) I think this is it . . Yes . . Yes . . Listen . . It's a poem . . Listen . .

> Often I think of afterlife.
> Of the living after living
> Often I think of life itself
> Of the dying where I stand.

> Bitter bitter bitter bitter
> Bitter bitter bitter bitter

. . That's the sound of the subway . . that's the chorus . . we . . we can do that together . . all right . . when I indicate we just say . . bitter . . like a lemon bitter . . over and over quickly . . all right . . all right?

SIDNEY

(*smiles*) All right . . (*shrugs*) If you want . .

JONATHAN

OK . . I'll start again . .

> Often I think of afterlife
> Of the living after living
> Often I think of life itself
> Of the dying where I stand.

All right . .

> Bitter bitter bitter bitter
> Bitter bitter bitter bitter
> Bitter bitter bitter bitter
> Bitter bitter bitter bitter.

The smoke from the sausage is starting to fill the room.

> And while I sway
> And while I move
> I calculate all the moving
> I have ever done,
> All the swaying I will do.

> Bitter bitter bitter bitter . .

All right . . now just keep that up in the background . . just keep saying it . .

SIDNEY

I think the sausage . .

JONATHAN

It's all right . . it's all right . . just go ahead.

SIDNEY

Well . . Bitter bitter . .

JONATHAN

That's it . . keep going . . (*Sidney sits and says the word over and over in back of Jonathan's lines. Jonathan gets very involved.*)

    . . All the swaying I will do . .

> For I will sway and I will
> Move and never see the sun
> And I will touch and I will
> Take and never understand
> And I will look and never find
> And I will find and never know
> And I will know and never use
> The movement I have made toward life.

He is now up ranting as she goes "bitter bitter" and the room fills with smoke.

> For I have seen trains rushing by
> And time and all that makes men move
> And yet
>
> Have felt that all this flow
> Was tapped from some far sterile stream.
>
> From some far sterile stream . .
> That turns the turbines of the world . .
> So all men move . . and never know . .
> That life and movement
> Never have
> Been aye the same.

SIDNEY

Jonathan . . the pan . . (*stops and rushes in to get the pan . . the smoke has filled the room*)

JONATHAN

> It moves the world
> And that is what must move.
> The world must move
> For life to be . .

SIDNEY

OOOOOH. (*screams, drops the pan*)

JONATHAN

The . . Whaa . . (*runs to her*) What happened?

SIDNEY

I BURNED myself . . the . . ah . . the pan's on the floor. (*he bends*) NO . . it's hot . . ah . . watch the sausage . . (*Jonathan gets a towel, picks up the pan, throws it in the sink, turns on the water: a gush of steam rises*)

JONATHAN

You all right . .

SIDNEY

Yes . . op– open the window . . (*Jonathan runs back and picks the sausage up and throws it in sink too*)

JONATHAN

What can I do . . for your burn . .

SIDNEY

It's all right . .

JONATHAN

Here . . here . . (*opens refrigerator, takes out butter*) Here . . rub that on . . it's oleo . . or something . . (*she does this*) You all right . . are you?

SIDNEY

Yes . . yes . .

JONATHAN

(*begins waving smoke out of room*) Boy . . A lot of smoke . . Come . . in here . . and we'll wait till it goes out . . And . . and I'll take you out for some dinner . .

SIDNEY

Is it all right . . all this smoke . .

JONATHAN

It won't hurt anybody . .

SIDNEY

Does Paul . . mind . . that you use the stuff . .

JONATHAN

No, Paul doesn't mind . . Paul is a brick . . Paul is . . You will meet him . . and then you will know . .

SIDNEY

You sure he doesn't mind . .

JONATHAN

I am sure . . drink up . .

SIDNEY

I'm fine . .

JONATHAN

OK . . (*they sit as the smoke clears, just sit, Jonathan drinking, musing. Sidney gets up and walks around the room examining things.*) Did you like my poem . .

SIDNEY

I . . don't know . . I couldn't tell . . it was confusing . .

JONATHAN

Mmmm . . well . . it's supposed to be . . in a way . . bitter . . bitter . . (*there is a pause again, while she walks and he sits*) Sidney?

SIDNEY

Eh?

JONATHAN

Do you know that I had a brother . .

SIDNEY

I know you have a brother . .

JONATHAN

No . . I had a younger brother . .

SIDNEY

Well . .

JONATHAN

I had a younger brother . . and he died . . you know . .

SIDNEY

Oh . .

JONATHAN

He was nine years old when he died . . Do you want to know how he died . .

SIDNEY

How . .

JONATHAN

He killed himself. He was nine years old and he committed suicide . . Do you believe that . .

SIDNEY

I guess so . . It's strange . .

JONATHAN

Yes . . I suppose it is . . But what is strange is why he did it . . Do you know why he did it . . I'll tell you why. He did it because he got a bad mark on a handwriting test in third grade . . He couldn't write very neatly and his teacher gave him a bad mark . .

SIDNEY

Why should he kill himself . .

JONATHAN

Because . . I think . . he was made a fool of . . I think his teacher told the class how sloppy his handwriting was . . and his report card gave him an unsatisfactory . . And he told my parents . . when he got it . . that he tried . . That . . he tried . . and then he got a bad mark . . and he hung himself in our cellar from his favorite pipe. A water pipe that he liked . . because it had a bump in it . . He came home from school one afternoon and left his paper on his bed and drank a glass of milk in the kitchen . . and went down to the cellar to his junk pile . . When my mother called him for dinner he didn't come . . My father cut him down . . I was only twelve . . and I remember that all I could think of was . . how did he know how to do that . . How did he know how to do it . . And now I wonder about a lot of things . . about that . . How old he must have been. In third grade, not to want to be made a fool of . . How hungry he must have been for respect. And love . . at his level . . If you had seen his junk pile you would have known that . . He saved . . he saved strange things . . he saved discarded hats . . and rubbers . . and things he could take care of . . And played games alone . . Sometimes with me . . but mostly alone. That's why no one missed him in the cellar until dinner. That's why. And he went right down and hung himself . . That's what the doctor said . . right down . . It's funny . .

SIDNEY

What's funny . .

JONATHAN

I always wonder why . . he drank his milk first . . What did he need that for . . Sidney . .

SIDNEY

Eh?

JONATHAN

Have . . you ever wanted to die . .

SIDNEY

I don't know . .

JONATHAN

Think about it . .

SIDNEY

I guess I have . .

JONATHAN

Oh . . I think I'd like to die . .

SIDNEY

You mean now . .

JONATHAN

I think so . . I don't know though . . and that's the problem . . it's nothing you can be unsure about. Once you're dead you can't change your mind.

SIDNEY

I guess not.

JONATHAN

Wouldn't you like to die?

SIDNEY

Now?

JONATHAN

Uh huh . .

SIDNEY

Well . . I don't think so . .

JONATHAN

How about . . if I said . . let's die together . . We could close all the windows . . and turn on the gas in here . . and . . it sounds very pleasant . . We'd never have to look for work . .

SIDNEY

Wouldn't . . we go to hell . .

JONATHAN

Well . . there's work *there*, shoveling coal, piling brimstone . .

SIDNEY

(*takes Jonathan's hand*) Jonathan . . (*kisses him on the cheek*) You make me laugh . .

JONATHAN

Couldn't we die together . . I mean . . we could jump off a bridge to-gether . . and go swooping down . . for . . one moment it would be magnificent . . Holding hands . . and charging down toward the water . . then pooosh . . and silence . . I'd like that very much, I think . . silence . . wouldn't you.

SIDNEY

I don't think I want to die yet . . I want to go back to school . .

JONATHAN

But you'll always want to go back to school . . That's the trouble . . Everybody's always a chapter ahead of me . . that's the trouble . . and you see . . you see . . I can go right to the end of the whole volume . .

the whole smacking volume . . if we just join hands . . and swish
. . silence . . (*she sits*) Do I scare you . .

SIDNEY

No . . you . . I don't know . .

JONATHAN

You know . . but you won't admit it . .

SIDNEY

What . .

JONATHAN

Nothing . . (*the door opens and Paul enters*)

PAUL

Whhhoop . . Hello . .

JONATHAN

Come in, come in . .

PAUL

"Joe sent me . ."

JONATHAN

You . . you don't know Sidney . . Sidney, this is Paul . .

PAUL

How are you . .

SIDNEY

Hello.

PAUL

It stinks in here . . what was burning . .

JONATHAN

Oh . . just some sausage . . We had a sausage burning . .

PAUL

Smells delicious . .

JONATHAN

I was going to make dinner for Sid —

PAUL

(*at sink*) You didn't quite make it . .

JONATHAN

Nope . .

PAUL

Jonathan . . the garbage goes into the garbage bag, not the sink . .
(*takes out sausage*) And you should have put some soap in the pan . .

JONATHAN

(*going to sink*) I'll clean it . .

PAUL

Not now . . not now . . just sometime . . You have a guest . .

JONATHAN

Ehhhh . . all right . . Would you like a drink?

PAUL

(*laughs*) No thank you, Jonathan . . would you?

JONATHAN

Ho ho . .

PAUL

(*going to closet to hang up coat*) I see you picked up your clothing . .

JONATHAN

Yes I . . did . .

PAUL

(*opens door and sees it piled in closet, turns to Jonathan*) Jonathan . . This isn't any better . .

JONATHAN

Oh . . ah . . (*goes to closet . . they both look at it, as a specimen*) Yes . . well . . (*bends over and takes the armful of clothing and trots off with it*)

PAUL

Where are you taking it . .

JONATHAN

I don't know . . ah . .

PAUL

Come here . . (*Jonathan spins around, tottering with armful of clothes*) What are you going to do with it . .

JONATHAN

That's a very good question . . What do you do with it . .

PAUL

Well . . once upon a time we could have hung it all up, couldn't we . .

JONATHAN

Ye-es . . that's true, professor . .

PAUL

But we didn't, did we . .

JONATHAN

Noo-ooo, professor . .

PAUL

So now we have an armful of it, don't we . .

JONATHAN

Ye-es professor . .

PAUL

And something must be done . .

JONATHAN

SOMETHING MUST BE DONE! I have it . . (*drops the pile*) Let's have a drink and think about it . .

PAUL

Jonathan . . wait . . (*goes into closet and gets a pillow case*) Here . . put the dirty stuff in here . . and hang the rest up . . (*Jonathan nods*) Next time I'm just going to throw the stuff out . .

JONATHAN

Yes . . yes . .

PAUL

(*wanders into where Sidney is, just sitting*) Hello . . Don't mind us while we play house . .

SIDNEY

All right . . Can . . I . . wash the pan . .

PAUL

No . . I'll do it . .

JONATHAN

Paul . . I think this sock is yours . .

PAUL

Well, shame on me . . Put it in my laundry bag . .

JONATHAN

Yes, shame on you . .

PAUL

Why didn't you tell me you were having dinner here . .

JONATHAN

Ohhh, it's all right . . I didn't know . . I met Sidney for lunch . . and you know one thing led to another . .

PAUL

Like dinner . .

JONATHAN

Like dinner . .

PAUL

How's your job, Sidney . . I hear you're ah . . sitting in a stall all day.

SIDNEY

Well . . I . . I'm not working there anymore . .

PAUL

No more free dance lessons . .

212

SIDNEY

No . .

JONATHAN

No . . She quit . . and we are now both in the same fraternity . . We are the welfare twins . .

PAUL

You can't get welfare unless you work . . Everybody in the unemployment line has worked . .

JONATHAN

Well, that's just as well . . I don't want to stand in line anyway . . Neither does Sidney. That's as bad as talking on the phone all day . .

PAUL

You don't *have* to work . . do you?

SIDNEY

No . . I guess not . . I do for money . . My money . . and . . (*shrugs*)

PAUL

And what . .

SIDNEY

And . . my parents . .

PAUL

You do for money and your parents . . That means?

SIDNEY

My parents . . want me to work . . They think it's good for me . .

PAUL

Oh . . Well, is it good for me?

SIDNEY

I don't know . .

PAUL

Well, what do you know . .

SIDNEY

I don't know . . I guess I like to work . . if I like the work . .

PAUL

She's particular like you . .

JONATHAN

Of course . . we're blood brothers. Say . . what happened today. You were supposed to call up NBC.

PAUL

Oh . . ah . . well nothing really.

JONATHAN

Did you call?

PAUL

Yeah . .

JONATHAN

. . and . .

PAUL

And nothing . .

JONATHAN

I thought you said they were all excited about the opera. They were going to show it to this other guy and . .

PAUL

And "this other guy" didn't particularly like it. So —

JONATHAN

So . .

PAUL

So, he told us to work on something seasonal.

JONATHAN

What does that mean . .

PAUL

Seasonal . . Christmas . . Easter . .

JONATHAN

So write a Christmas opera.

PAUL

We would, except . . I doubt if he really means it . . Instead of just saying . . We don't do operas on television . . they lead you on . . Now it's seasonal, next it'll be something else . . Look . . they don't do plays anymore . . they aren't going to do a short opera.

JONATHAN

Paul writes the libretto . . and Jeff . . you know Jeff Levine from school.

SIDNEY

No . .

JONATHAN

He writes the music . . It's lovely . . lovely . . that's it . . You write a Christmas opera . . a Christmas opera with music by Levine . . Somebody has to buy that . .

PAUL

Nobody *has* to buy nothin' . . except this . . (*holds up record*) And

now ladies and gentlemen . . here we are with Renata Tebaldi singing . . "Baby Don't Go Home."

JONATHAN

Come on, we'll go out and eat.

PAUL

With what . .

JONATHAN

With ah . . Sidney has something . .

PAUL

I'll just get a few things . .

JONATHAN

Look, you've eaten already . . haven't you. So just sit . . down and
we'll eat later. We can always eat . . I want you to sit and drink with us
and enjoy our company . . and tell Sidney about your Christmas or
Easter opera or something . . (*goes to get another drink*)

PAUL

Watch it, Jonathan . . just watch . .

JONATHAN

I'm quite all right. I'm quite all right. You — you — you tell Sidney about
your opera . . and then I'll tell you what I decided to do today. Do you
know what I am going to do?

PAUL

No, what am you going to do?

JONATHAN

I am going back to Italy. I am going to go back and tear down the Via
Veneto and tear into the cloisters of my old church and say, "Chaplain
. . I have returned. Let's have a drink!"

PAUL

And where do you get the money for the trip?

JONATHAN

It's a riddle, isn't it. I want to go to Italy, but I need money, so I must
work, but I can't get a job, so I want to go to Italy, but I can't go without
money so I must, etc. . . . etc. . . . etc. . .

PAUL

Jonathan . .

JONATHAN

I have it. I'll join the mafia and they'll *deport* me!

PAUL

Jonathan . . have a seat . . I have an idea . .

JONATHAN

Yes . . you have an idea . .

PAUL

What happened to Father Wagoner . .

JONATHAN

Well . . I don't think there's much there . .

PAUL

You were going to ask him about the job at the church . . for the quarterly.

JONATHAN

Oh . . Father Wagoner . . I don't know . .

PAUL

You could talk to him . .

JONATHAN

I suppose I could.

PAUL

Do that.

JONATHAN

Yes . . I don't know . . You know . . I saw a man today in the park playing a guitar . . It was wonderful . . I'd love to be able to play a guitar . . just have a guitar . . and myself and that would be all . . No office . . No typewriter . . Just a guitar and myself . .

PAUL

And the ability . .

JONATHAN

The perseverance . . If I could take a year . . and just play . . Then . . I couldn't do anything . . huh . . You know . . Paul . . I was talking to Sidney at lunch. I told Sidney at lunch . . (*going to get another drink*)

PAUL

Don't, Jonathan . . I'll have to pick you up . .

JONATHAN

It's all right . .

PAUL

It's not all right! You have a guest.

JONATHAN

Just a teeny, teeny . . You know . . I told . . Sidney at lunch . . that I saw that man . . Do you know . . Do you know that I am going to marry Sidney . .

PAUL

Congratulations . .

JONATHAN

Don't you think we'd make a good couple . . Sidney is going to marry me some day . . aren't you, Sidney . .

SIDNEY

I don't know . . Jonathan . .

JONATHAN

Well she doesn't know, but she knows. She is the only love I have . .

PAUL

Currently . .

JONATHAN

Yes . . currently . . No . . no not currently . . do you know at lunch, I decided what I was going to do . .

PAUL

What's that . .

JONATHAN

Tonight I am going to bed . . and tomorrow I'm going to get up . . and walk over the bridge and stick out my thumb and I'm going to Mexico . . Tomorrow I am going to go to Mexico . .

PAUL

No you're not, Jonathan . .

JONATHAN

No I'm not . . (*laughs*) . . No I'm not . . Ohhhhhhhhhh (*sits and laughs*) . . Are you hungry, my dear . .

SIDNEY

I'm all right . . I'm not too hungry . .

JONATHAN

Well, I'll get you something . .

PAUL

I said I'd go out . .

JONATHAN

No, I want to go out . .

PAUL

Stay with Sidney, I'll go out . .

JONATHAN

No, I want you to stay . . you're a lovely couple . . I want you to tell Sidney about your opera . . You're a lovely couple . . (*Jonathan and Paul are up*)

217

PAUL

Look, let *me* go . .

JONATHAN

No . . I'm off. (*starts to door*)

PAUL

Jonathan, you don't have any money . . now come here . .

JONATHAN

I'm going . .

PAUL

You don't even know where to go . .

JONATHAN

(*opens door, turns*) Oh yes I do . . I'm going out . . I'm going to kill myself. (*He slams the door . . and his fast footsteps are heard going down the stairs. Sidney is up but Paul stops her.*)

SIDNEY

He's going . . You'd better get him . .

PAUL

He's all right . . I'm used to it . .

SIDNEY

But he said . . well . .

PAUL

Don't worry, he'll be back . . he gets this way . . you should know . .

SIDNEY

Ehh, but . . We were talking before . . Paul . . We were talking about that before . . about killing ourselves . . himself . . oh . .

PAUL

What . .

SIDNEY

Before, before you came . . He said he wanted to kill himself . . He asked me . . to jump off a bridge with him . .

PAUL

When . .

SIDNEY

Before you came . . he talked about it before you came . .

PAUL

(*looks at door*) Well . . well . . he'll be back . .

SIDNEY

How do you know . . he . . drank a lot . .

PAUL

He always comes back . .

218

SIDNEY

You don't think anything will happen . .

PAUL

Sidney . . a man once told me . . that anyone who kills himself is already dead . . before he does it . . (*Sidney just sits, distraught. Paul goes to refrigerator, opens it, pulls out ice tray.*) Goddamnit . . Why can't he put the ice away . . (*puts it back, gets drink, adds water in sink, and sits by Sidney*) He'll be back . . don't worry . . he still has . . all those stories . . and you . . ah . . know him pretty well . .

SIDNEY

Yes . . I guess . .

PAUL

Well then . .

SIDNEY

But . . he never talked like he did with me . . about dying together . .

PAUL

Well . . we all talk about it once . .

SIDNEY

We all aren't Jonathan . .

PAUL

No . . no . . Look . . Sidney . . He's been here for a while . . He'll be all right . . I know him . .

SIDNEY

All right. (*shrugs*)

PAUL

Are you hungry . .

SIDNEY

No . . I don't know . .

PAUL

What do you know . .

SIDNEY

I'm not hungry . .

PAUL

OK, let's stick with that . . What do you know about Jonathan . .

SIDNEY

Just enough . . I love Jonathan . . well not love-love but . . you know . .

PAUL

Yes . . I guess so . . He . . feels the same way . . He talks about you quite a lot . . I was curious . . you know . .

219

SIDNEY

Well . . If you think he talks about me . . You should hear him about you . .

PAUL

Yeah . . well . .

SIDNEY

He's been wanting me to meet you . . Every day he talks about you . . He thinks a lot of you . . He thinks you are going to be great, he says . .

PAUL

If only Jonathan were the prophet . . Jonathan believes in the old saying . . thinking makes it so . . well . . Ah . . You going to get another job?

SIDNEY

I don't . . know . . I really don't . . if I find one I like . . I have to be home before eleven . .

PAUL

Oh?

SIDNEY

I have to be home . .

PAUL

We'll wait . . for Jonathan . . for a while . .

SIDNEY

Can we look for him . .

PAUL

In a while . . give him time . . (*There is a long silence . . the two just sit. Paul looks at Sidney, and she looks away.*)

SIDNEY

Uhhhhh . .

PAUL

Yes?

SIDNEY

Can I . . uh . . have a glass of water . .

PAUL

Sure . . (*rises and goes to sink to pour water, returns to find Sidney rubbing her head as though she has a headache*) What's the matter . .

SIDNEY

Nothing . .

PAUL

You want some aspirin . .

SIDNEY

No . . I'm all right.

PAUL

Here . .

SIDNEY

Thank you . .

PAUL

You're a very attractive girl . . Why don't you . . help yourself out . .

SIDNEY

Huh . .

PAUL

Why don't you help yourself out . . you know . . fix your hair . .

SIDNEY

I don't care . .

PAUL

You should care . . you're attractive . .

SIDNEY

Thank you . .

PAUL

Ahhh . . Sidney . . Look . . Tell me something . . Tell me what *you* think about something . . Jonathan tells me about you . . but . . you don't help.

SIDNEY

There's . . nothing . . to tell . . you know . .

PAUL

You left school . .

SIDNEY

Yes . .

PAUL

You had something wrong . .

SIDNEY

Ehhhhhh, rheumatic fever . .

PAUL

Then what . .

SIDNEY

I came here . .

PAUL

And . .

SIDNEY

I don't know . . a couple of jobs . . my parents want me to live at home so they can watch that I don't get sick again . .

PAUL

Are you going back to school . .

SIDNEY

I don't know . .

PAUL

MY GOD, woman . . What exactly do you know? (*Sidney shrugs*) Look, you are an attractive girl . . And I'm sure there is something ticking inside of you . . in fact I know there is . . Look at me . . Look . . You have lovely gray eyes . . and there is something ticking in there . . and you only let one thousandth of it out . . Now why do you do that. That's not fair, is it . .

SIDNEY

I don't know . . I guess . .

PAUL

You guess what . .

SIDNEY

I guess not . .

PAUL

Well then do something, talk to me . .

SIDNEY

About what. I don't know anything . .

PAUL

Say something . . Tell me how you feel about this apartment . . Do you like this room . .

SIDNEY

It's all right . .

PAUL

It's all right, what kind of a comment is that. It's all right good . . it's all right bad . . it smells . . it's lovely . . it's decadent . . it's what . . Tell me . . tell me what you think about your parents . . tell me about the job . . look . . I like your face . . do you know . . I like your face . . Now talk to me . .

SIDNEY

What about . .

PAUL

I told you . . How do you like my apartment . .

SIDNEY

How do you?

PAUL

Oh God . . Answer me. Don't ask me . .

SIDNEY

Why not . .

PAUL

Because I want to find out about you . .

SIDNEY

Well . . I want to find out about you . .

PAUL

Well, say something and I'll join in and you'll find out . .

SIDNEY

Well, say something . .

PAUL

But you won't join in . . You'll sit there on your end of the log . . and . . say . . I don't know . . (*Sidney shrugs*) Now look . . Tell me what you think of the apartment . . tell me . .

SIDNEY

It's all right, I said . .

PAUL

No . . tell me . . describe everything . . and give an opinion . .

SIDNEY

I don't know . .

PAUL

Talk.

SIDNEY

I . . well . . it's . .

PAUL

Talk . .

SIDNEY

It's . .

PAUL

Talk . .

SIDNEY

I can't . .

PAUL

Look, don't think . . OK . . just . . say the first thing that comes into your mind . . here . . Lamp . . OK . . lamp . . Talk . .

SIDNEY

I can't . .

PAUL

Lamp . . lamp . . do you like it . .

SIDNEY

I don't know . .

PAUL

Do you like it . .

SIDNEY

Eh . . yes . .

PAUL

Why . .

SIDNEY

It's . .

PAUL

Why?

SIDNEY

It's . . ah . .

PAUL

Why . .

SIDNEY

It's . . it's . .

PAUL

It's what . .

SIDNEY

It's funny . .

PAUL

Good, it's funny . . it's what . .

SIDNEY

It's funny, it's — it's . . little and funny . . and the shade is too big for the lamp . . and and it's brown and gold and it's . . kind of ugly . . and . .

PAUL

Talk . .

SIDNEY

And ugly . . and funny . . and . . but ugly like it's pretty and . .

PAUL

Chair . . chair .

SIDNEY

Well, the chair is . . a nice chair . .

PAUL

Talk . .

SIDNEY

Its stuffing is coming out, but it looks comfortable and the kind of chair you might want to sit in and . . (*they speak simultaneously*)

SIDNEY	PAUL
The cover is kind of ugly but once I guess it was all right and it looks like a chair I used to sit in at school . . and like a chair my grandmother used to have . . and . . a . . it was very comfortable . . it looks . . it looks, it looks like a very comfortable chair . . that I don't think you should get rid of even though it's falling apart because it looks like it is lived in and very comfortable and it probably came from the Salvation Army and from someone . . who had it and maybe it was my grandmother and maybe you could fix it up . . and . . and . . and I don't know . . and that painting is nice . . It looks . . it looks like an old man and a dog and it looks like the man likes his dog but the dog doesn't like the man as much because he has a sad expression on his face . . but it's a nice painting . . I like the way it's done . . it's . . it's a wash . . and I like the way it's done except that the dog is sad and I don't like sad dogs . . I guess . . I don't know . . maybe it's just the way I look at it . . and . . and . . the chair, I said, the chair, it's a comfortable chair . . an' the floor, the coffee table is old . . and it's old and	Talk . . go ahead . . Talk . . it looks . . Talk . . anything . . talk . . The painting . . Keep going . . Talk . . Keep going . .

225

I don't know . . This is . . I can't keep going . . This is . . I talked about . . that it's . . I don't know . . I am. I am . . I can't just talk . . It's what . . It's . . what . . I can't just . . You're Paul . . You're Paul . . You're Paul . . You're Paul . . You're . . I don't know . . I don't know . . I can't . . I . . I . . I . . ehhhh.

No, keep going . . The chair, then, the chair . . Talk . .

(*sitting beside her*) Who am I . . You're attractive . . Who am I . . Talk . . Tell me something . .

She again holds her head down as if it hurts. Paul takes hold of her head, lifts her face toward him. There are tears running down her face.

PAUL

I'm sorry . . (*He holds her face and they look at each other. He kisses, then releases her.*) You don't kiss either, do you . . I'm sorry . . What's the matter?

SIDNEY

Uh huhhhhh.

PAUL

What does that mean .

SIDNEY

It's nothing . . I . . I get upset . . It's nothing . .

PAUL

What . .

SIDNEY

Please . . I don't want to tell you.

PAUL

All right . . Did you tell Jonathan?

SIDNEY

It's nothing . . It's just about my job . . I quit my job and my parents don't know . . that's all . . I'll get another . .

PAUL

And you'll go back to school . .

SIDNEY

I hope so . .

PAUL

You told that to Jonathan . .

SIDNEY

Yes . . he knows . . but . .

PAUL

But what . .

SIDNEY

But . . I don't know . .

PAUL

Don't say that to me . . but what?

SIDNEY

But . . ehhhhh . . (*She rises. She is strangely inept, just crosses and sits in the stuffed chair. She breathes heavily, then begins to cry. Bends over and cries.*)

PAUL

(*goes to her*) What . .

SIDNEY

Jonathan . . doesn't know . .

PAUL

What . . tell me . . what is the matter . . Don't sit there by yourself . . Do you want to tell me . . (*Sidney shakes "No," continues crying. Paul kneels, waits, then rises and goes back and sits and waits. She continues crying, then stops. Sits up. They sit and look across at each other. Paul rises, goes to bureau, gets handkerchief, crosses to her, and offers it. She takes it. Then just about to wipe, she moans.*)

SIDNEY

Ohhhhh noo . .

PAUL

(*is really bewildered*) Jesus . .

SIDNEY

Paul . . I have to go home . . I have to go home. (*rises and starts right to the door*)

PAUL

(*intercepts her*) Not until you tell me what is wrong . .

SIDNEY

I can't.

PAUL

It's Jonathan . . is it Jonathan . .

SIDNEY

No . . Yes . .

PAUL

You're still worried about Jonathan.

SIDNEY

No . . It's . .

227

PAUL

It's what . . FOR GOD'S SAKE SAY SOMETHING . .

SIDNEY

It's . . I can't tell Jonathan . . I want to tell Jonathan, but I can't tell Jonathan.

PAUL

WHAT . . YOU CAN'T TELL JONATHAN WHAT . .

SIDNEY

I can't . .

PAUL

What, for God's sake, what . .

SIDNEY

I . . I . . left school . . because . . because . .

PAUL

What?

SIDNEY

. . because I had a baby . . (*lets go and Paul holds her*)

PAUL

Sit . . sit down . . (*sits her down on couch*) Just take it easy . .

SIDNEY

I . . I . . didn't want to tell him I didn't have rheumatic fever . . and . . I was in school . . till I was bursting . . I had to tell my parents . . and I was in the hospital here . . and I had the child . . and we gave it away . . And my parents want me home to watch me . . I have to prove myself responsible . . they have to watch me . . And . .

PAUL

Was it Jonathan . . the child's . .

SIDNEY

No. No . . no . . It was a boy at school . . Just some boy . . I didn't even know . . which boy . .

PAUL

Oh . . Oh . .

SIDNEY

I don't even know . . I have to go . .

PAUL

No . . you stay . . it's early . . Stay and talk . .

SIDNEY

I can't tell Jonathan . .

PAUL

Then you won't . . it's all right . .

228

SIDNEY

I want to go back to school . .

PAUL

Then you will . .

SIDNEY

But I have to be home . .

PAUL

Look . . one thing at a time . . one thing . . OK? OK?

SIDNEY

OK . .

PAUL

Did you love this boy . .

SIDNEY

No . . he was just someone . .

PAUL

Of many . .

SIDNEY

Of . . many . . of . . I don't sleep with everyone . . I liked him
. . I . . but . .

PAUL

Yes . .

SIDNEY

That's all . .

PAUL

Look, take it easy . . just take it easy . . OK?

SIDNEY

OK . .

PAUL

Wipe your eyes.

SIDNEY

OK . . (*She sits and wipes her eyes. Paul goes and refills her water
glass.*)

PAUL

Drink this . . and take it easy . . take it easy . . It's off your chest
. . so take it easy . . (*she sits, wipes, and adjusts herself to composure*)
You all right . .

SIDNEY

Uh huh . .

PAUL

Was it worth all that . .

SIDNEY

I guess not . . It's silly . .

PAUL

Why is it silly . .

SIDNEY

Because . . because . . other people know . . just . . some people don't know.

PAUL

Oh . .

SIDNEY

Peter knows . .

PAUL

Peter's slept with you?

SIDNEY

No . . No, he knows . .

PAUL

Peter's slept with you.

SIDNEY

No, he hasn't . . He has tried . . but I don't like Peter because Peter is always an animal and is never just someone I can like . . Even with my parents . . he performs . . He performs as the perfect gentleman . . and he is so handsome . . and so everything . . and you must fall at his feet . . but he doesn't even wait for you to fall . . he gets you on your way down . . and Peter doesn't like me for that . . because I don't care about him . . and he never gives up . .

PAUL

Well, you talked . .

SIDNEY

I was sure it was a — a matter of time before he told Jonathan and I decided it didn't matter. It's just that if you have some people . . who care about you . . why take a chance . .

PAUL

Would Jonathan care any less . .

SIDNEY

Why take a chance . .

PAUL

How much do you care about Jonathan?

SIDNEY

I told you.

PAUL

The baby's father . . How much did you care about him?

SIDNEY

He was just someone . . Someone I met . . I just met him one night . .

PAUL

Like me . .

SIDNEY

Yes . .

PAUL

And that was enough . .

SIDNEY

I just . . I don't have to love someone do I . . I just liked him . .

PAUL

Who did you ever love?

SIDNEY

No one . . no . . one . . I can remember . . I don't think I ever will . .

PAUL

You don't care . .

SIDNEY

I don't care . .

PAUL

But you'd care . .

SIDNEY

No, I don't care . .

PAUL

If you went back to school would you care . .

SIDNEY

I don't know . .

PAUL

If you got a job . . If your parents let you go . . If Peter let you alone . . If something strange happened that you liked . .

SIDNEY

I'm strange . . that's the only strange thing . .

PAUL

You're strange . . by your request . . Look . . Why don't you . . try . . just once . . to just give in to someone . .

SIDNEY

I don't know what that means.

231

PAUL

You don't . .

SIDNEY

You want me to sleep with you . .

PAUL

Only if you want to . .

SIDNEY

But that's what you want, isn't it?

PAUL

I want you to give in to me . . Like before . . when you told me something . . like that . .

SIDNEY

I'm sorry . . I got . . I get like that . .

PAUL

Don't be sorry . . Get like that again . . I don't mind . .

SIDNEY

You like people to cry all over you . . You want me to move in too?

PAUL

That's not nice . .

SIDNEY

I'm not nice . .

PAUL

You are strange . . and you are not nice . . What else are you . .

SIDNEY

I'm psycho . .

PAUL

Oh . . OK . . we'll add that to the list . .

SIDNEY

OK . .

PAUL

OK . . You're a mother, aren't you . .

SIDNEY

Huh . .

PAUL

You're a mother . . So you did give something . .

SIDNEY

I gave it away . . We gave the baby away . .

PAUL

Did you see it . .

SIDNEY

I carried it for nine months . . That was enough . .

PAUL

You're funny you know . . You're very funny . . First you don't talk
. . then you cry . . then you talk . . then you get arrogant . . When
do you give up . .

SIDNEY

I don't know what you're talking about . .

PAUL

When do you give up . . (*she turns away*) Who are you? Hey . . look
at me . . Hey . . (*takes her head and turns it toward him*) Hey . .
(*They just stare at each other, his two hands holding her face firmly, then
slowly, slowly, she brings one hand up and rests it on top of one of his.
She takes the hand from her face and presses it to her lips.*) Sidney . . it's
all right . . I like you. I like you . . Do you believe me . . (*Sidney
shrugs*) I want an answer, Sidney . . Do you believe me. Sidney . .

SIDNEY

Yes . . I guess . . I do . .

PAUL

No guessing . . Do you believe me . . (*she looks at him again . .
then lets her head fall against him as her eyes grow wet*) You're not going to cry again . . (*she shakes her head "No"*) Then stop . . (*Sidney
nods. He takes her face and kisses her.*) Look . . I want you to kiss me
. . You are a human being . . You understand . . (*she shakes "No,"
smiles*) OK . . (*kisses her cheek . . and she turns to brush him, then
again picks up his hand and kisses it*) Thank you . . that's a start . .
that's a good start . . (*takes her by the shoulders and pulls her to him;
they lie back on the couch, her head resting on his chest*) Hear my heart
. . one . . two . . three . . four . .

SIDNEY

(*suddenly sits up*) I have to go . .

PAUL

What . .

SIDNEY

I have to be home by eleven . .

PAUL

Why do you have to be home . .

SIDNEY

I told you my parents . . (*starts to get up*) I have to be home by eleven
. . (*is up*)

PAUL

(*goes after her and takes her by the shoulders*) Why?

SIDNEY

You know why.

PAUL

Why.

SIDNEY

My parents . .

PAUL

They have to watch you . .

SIDNEY

Yes . .

PAUL

To make sure you don't sleep with anybody else . .

SIDNEY

Yes . .

PAUL

All right . . (*taking her over to couch and sitting her down*)

SIDNEY

What . . I have to go . . what . .

PAUL

What do you want to do . .

SIDNEY

I have to be home . .

PAUL

What do you want to do . .

SIDNEY

I have . .

PAUL

Goddamnit, answer the question?

SIDNEY

I . . want to go home . .

PAUL

All right . . go . .

SIDNEY

My parents . .

PAUL

Look . . isn't this silly . . Isn't this the most ridiculous goddamn thing
in the world . . It's nine o'clock . . You don't think you could get
screwed in two hours . . and then run home . . You don't think that
could happen . .

SIDNEY

I don't know . .

PAUL

You don't, huh . .

SIDNEY

Yes, I guess so . .

PAUL

Well then . . what's the matter with you . .

SIDNEY

I want to go to school . .

PAUL

And I want you to give yourself up to somebody . . I think that's more
important right now . .

SIDNEY

I told you I'd sleep with you . . I don't care . .

PAUL

But I do care . .

SIDNEY

I don't understand you . . I have to go . .

PAUL

Look . . For Christ's sake . . Just stop . . stop . . and say to yourself . . I like it here . . I like it here . . I don't care what anybody
thinks . . I am here with someone who says he likes me . . who doesn't
care about anything else . . For God's sake . . Just stay . . and talk
. . and breathe and think and cry or stand on your head . . But give it
time . . give it time to grow . . up . . down . . anywhere . . I'm
not Jonathan . . I'm not Peter . . I'm someone else . . and I want to
know you . . you're going to know me . .

SIDNEY

My parents . .

PAUL

Can go screw themselves . . They've got you all wound up . . like this
. . (*holds up fist*) Like this . . Now . . Here . . Kiss . . (*holds out*

fist to her; she sits) Kiss . . (*Sidney leans forward and kisses his fist*) Shazam . . (*slowly unfolds fist to a full relaxed hand; she looks and looks at it and Paul smiles*) Good girl . . (*as she reaches out to take his hand lights fade and out, and curtain*)

Scene 2

Apartment. The next morning, late. Paul's bed is unmade after a night's sleep. Paul is alone on stage. He is shaving with an electric shaver in the mirror over his bureau. He is dressed in casual khaki pants, a T-shirt, and some slippers. He continues shaving. The bathroom door opens. Sidney comes out in a bathrobe much too large for her.

PAUL
Shower work all right?
SIDNEY
Yes . . Gets hot and cold though . . you know . .
PAUL
You burn yourself . .
SIDNEY
Almost . .
PAUL
You hungry . .
SIDNEY
I don't know . .
PAUL
AH, AH, AHH! *Are you hungry?*
SIDNEY
A little . .
PAUL
Well I have to get some milk . . and eggs . . I'll run down to the deli . . (*finishes shaving, starts dressing*)
SIDNEY
That's all right . . I'll just have coffee . .
PAUL
Well I won't . . so I'll run down . .
SIDNEY
No . . call . . from Jonathan . .

PAUL

No . . maybe he's at Peter's . . He has gone to Peter's before . .

SIDNEY

Maybe . .

PAUL

I'll check at the bars in the neighborhood when I go out . . I'll see if he was there . . If he drank enough . . He's all right . .

SIDNEY

Does . . he stay out a lot . .

PAUL

Yes . . but . . he usually comes back . . unless he's with Peter . . Or . . He's all right . . Look, there's real coffee in the cabinet . . why don't you make some . . instead of the instant crap . . and it'll be all ready when I get back . .

SIDNEY

How do you make it . .

PAUL

You're kidding . .

SIDNEY

No . . I never made coffee . . (*shrugs*)

PAUL

Look . . (*leads her to kitchen area*) Here . . Here is the coffee, see? . . Now . . We open the coffeepot . . and we take out the insides . . see . . And we take the coffee down from the cabinet, see? (*takes down can*) And we open it . . And we shovel spoonfuls of coffee into the little silver cylinder, see . . and when they reach . . about . . here . . we stop . . and we put on the lid . . and then we fill the pot with water . . up to . . let's see . . four cups . . (*runs water*) there . . then we put the insides back inside . . and we put the top on. Then what . .

SIDNEY

(*shrugs*) Light the stove . .

PAUL

Very good . . go ahead . . (*she does*) And put the pot on . . (*she does*) *Bene! Bene!* Now next time you have to make coffee you know what to do . .

SIDNEY

I guess so . .

PAUL

When it perks for about ten minutes . . take it off . . All right?

SIDNEY

Perks . .

PAUL

You know . . blub . . blub . . blub . .

SIDNEY

Eh huh . .

PAUL

You'll smell it . . (*putting on coat*)

SIDNEY

OK . .

PAUL

So now you're all set . . When I come back we'll learn how to boil water . . all right?

SIDNEY

I can do that . .

PAUL

Oh . . All right . . then we'll fry eggs . . and . . I'll bet I know something else you can't do that I can . . (*at door*) Burn toast . . Can you burn toast . .

SIDNEY

I don't know . .

PAUL

If you say no . . you're hired . .

SIDNEY

No . .

PAUL

Hired . . see you later. (*He goes out and closes door. Sidney, alone, crosses to phonograph and puts on a record. She listens for a moment, then goes back to kitchen to take a look at the coffeepot. Then, she takes a kitchen chair, puts it in front of the stove, and sits and watches the coffee perk. Satisfied that it's doing all right, she gets up and goes to make the bed. Knock on door.*)

SIDNEY

(*stops*) Yes . . (*Peter enters*)

PETER

It was open . . well . . Good morning to you, Mary Sunshine . . Early party . . Late party . . What?

SIDNEY

Nothing . . nothing . .

PETER

Can I have the next dance . .

SIDNEY

No, it's . . no . . I . . (*crosses to phonograph and turns it off*)

PETER

Ahhhhhh. That's nice music . . leave it on . .

SIDNEY

It's not mine . .

PETER

Eh . . You stay here last night . .

SIDNEY

Eh . . I ah . . What do you want . .

PETER

I guess so huh . . So Jonathan joins the club . . That's nice . . You look good in his robe . . very nice . . That the club uniform . . It's about time . .

SIDNEY

Peter! Where's Jonathan . .

PETER

Peter where's Jonathan?

SIDNEY

Where's Jonathan . .

PETER

Don't you think you ought to know . .

SIDNEY

Jonathan . . Oh no . .

PETER

Go ahead . . go ahead . .

SIDNEY

No . .

PETER

Go ahead . . I'm going to find out . . so go ahead . .

SIDNEY

Jonathan . . ran out last night . . after drinking . . and . . he said he was going to kill himself . .

PETER

And you've been here waiting . . That's screwy . . he just said that, for Christ's sake.

SIDNEY

He didn't just say it, Peter . . We had a long talk . . well a talk about
it . . He didn't just say it . .

PETER

Oh . . well . .

SIDNEY

We thought he might have gone over to your place . .

PETER

Who thought . .

SIDNEY

I thought . . he might . .

PETER

Where's Paul . .

SIDNEY

He . . went out . . to look for Jonathan . .

PETER

Ehhh . . You ah . . You alone here last night . .

SIDNEY

(*shrugs*) Ehhh . . It's none of your business . . (*Peter laughs*) Do you
always just . . barge in . .

PETER

No, not always . .

SIDNEY

Well . . why don't you . . never mind . .

PETER

What . . what . . Look . . (*goes to her*) Look . . I never did anything to you, huh? . . I think I treat you very well . . I never hurt you,
huh . . I get your parents to spring you so you can go up to school for
a weekend . . So you can screw around up at school . . right? . .
Now why do I bug you . . huh . . Look . . I'm not a bad-looking
guy . . huh . . I think you're probably pretty good in bed, huh . .
what the hell . . I'm not going to hurt you. (*takes her by the shoulders*)

SIDNEY

Peter . . (*tries to free herself*)

PETER

Come on . . Just . . Give me a little rhythm huh . . come on . .
We'll . . We'll . . just grind it a little . . huh . .

SIDNEY

Peter, please . .

PETER

For Christ's sake . . I'm not going to kill you . . Come on, baby. (*He holds her and tries to kiss her and she keeps pulling away. He finally takes her in a great hug, putting his hand on her rear and kissing her neck; he tries to force her closer to him.*) Come on . . (*She makes resisting noises, and they grapple. The door opens. Paul enters.*)

PAUL

Hey "screwhead" . . How about it! (*Peter stops and lets go and backs off. Sidney runs into the bathroom.*) Sidney . . Sidney . . Where . . Sidney! You are the funniest man alive . . you know that . . What the hell is the matter with you.

PETER

Ah . . I wasn't going to hurt her . .

PAUL

What were you going to do . . for God's sake, you're not a sex maniac . . Can't you control yourself . .

PETER

Eh, that girl bugs me . . She goes down for the whole eastern United States . . everybody but me . .

PAUL

Look, I want you to keep your filthy mouth out of here, understand . . If you want to come up here . . then just keep your filthy mouth out . .

PETER

Oh, for Christ's sake . . It's all right if you make it, huh? But I come in to get my licks . . that's something different.

PAUL

Goddamnit Peter . . The day you take five minutes . . just five minutes with a girl to think about other things than putting her down . . then you can tell me about what I do . .

PETER

You can screw her; I can't . .

PAUL

Don't tell me what I did . . Don't walk in here and tell me . .

PETER

Ah come off it . .

PAUL

I've been with that girl since seven o'clock last night . . And I know one hell of a lot . . One hell of a lot . .

PETER

Yeah . . Tell me . . sing me . .

PAUL

Shall I tell you why you can't touch her . .

PETER

Give her time . . She just likes it . .

PAUL

Shall I tell you why you can't touch her . .

PETER

Give her time . . She just likes it . .

PAUL

Shall I tell you why you can't touch her . .

PETER

Give her time . .

PAUL

Shall I tell you . .

PETER

Oh screw . . tell me . . tell me. I'm dying . . I really give a shit . . I could care less . . (*Paul laughs*) So tell me . . go ahead, screw-head . .

PAUL

You hit it, friend . . You know the magic answer . .

PETER

OK . . OK . . funny man . . tell me . .

PAUL

You know yourself . .

PETER

Yeah?

PAUL

You could care less . .

PETER

Ehhhhhhhhhhhh. (*exasperated, turns away; Paul goes to bathroom door and knocks*)

PAUL

Sidney . . Sidney . . you all right . . Sidney . . (*opens slowly*) Come on . . come on out . . Come on . . (*goes into bathroom, speaks from within*) Come on . . I've got breakfast . . We've got to eat . . And you forgot the coffee . . it's perking . . (*they enter*) Go take the coffee off . . and we'll have breakfast. (*she goes to stove, turns off light, takes off coffee, and takes down cups while Paul puts milk away and takes eggs out of bag)*

PETER

Look . . I'm sorry . . For Christ's sake . . How about it . .

PAUL

You want some breakfast . .

PETER

I ate . .

PAUL

OK . . Jonathan . . didn't see you last night . .

PETER

No, what is this . . Sidney . . said something about . . killing himself . .

PAUL

Yes . . when he left . .

PETER

Well you know Jonathan . .

PAUL

Well, Peter . . I've always said yes . . I know Jonathan . . but one day we're going to be standing here making breakfast and be saying . . "well you know Jonathan" . . and he's going to be killing himself . . So . .

PETER

Ehhhhh . . we all say it . .

PAUL

What have you got to lose . .

PETER

I've said it . .

PAUL

You've got a lot to lose . . At least you think you do . . and that's the difference . .

PETER

I'll believe it when I see it . . Did you call Tubby . .

PAUL

I don't know Tubby's number . .

PETER

He could be at Tubby's . . He could be around the corner . . at the Avenue . .

PAUL

I stopped there . . he wasn't . .

PETER

Yeah . . well don't worry . . You . . ah, you want to go up to school . . there's a hockey match today . . (*Paul begins making the eggs; Sidney has poured the coffee*)

SIDNEY

Sugars?

PAUL

Two . . Coffee . . Peter . .

PETER

Yeah . . no sugar . . (*she brings him coffee*) I'm sorry . . huh . . huh . . You want to see the hockey match . .

SIDNEY

No . . thank you . .

PETER

You . .

PAUL

No . . I . . don't . . I have . . work . .

PETER

OK . . OK . . I'll wait for Jonathan . . I'll wait awhile . . (*Paul goes back to sink*)

PAUL

Just watch the eggs . . if they get brown turn the light off . . I want to empty the garbage . . smells . .

SIDNEY

Brown where . .

PAUL

That's all right . . I won't be a minute . . (*takes garbage bag and goes to the door; to Peter*) Can I trust you?

PETER

I'm a maniac . . I'm a maniac . .

PAUL

OK . . (*He opens the door; there is Jonathan. He wavers and then falls forward.*) Holy Christ . . (*drops the bag and catches the body, with Peter running to help him*) Get him on the couch . . come . .

PETER

What's the matter with him . .

SIDNEY

Jonathan . . what's the matter with him.

PAUL

Christ, maybe he's dead . . I don't know . . He weighs a ton . . You

244

weigh a ton when you're dead. (*they get him on couch*) Maybe he's dead . .

PETER

He's stoned, that's all.

PAUL

He's white . . Look at him. Jonathan . . (*shaking him*) Jonathan . . Jonathan, are you dead? Jonathan, are you dead . .

SIDNEY

What's the matter?

PETER

You don't ask a guy if he's dead or not . .

PAUL

Jonathan . . Jonathan . . For Christ's sake . . Jonathan, are you dead?

PETER

You don't ask a guy if he's dead!

PAUL

Well this one you do . . This one you do! (*he continues, touching his face, saying his name, as they look at him*) Jonathan . . Jonathan . . Are you dead . . Jonathan?

JONATHAN

Yes . . I'm dead! (*black out and curtain*)

ACT THREE

The apartment. The following evening. Paul sits in chair reading the paper as the phonograph is playing church music, a kyrie. The phone rings. Paul waits, lets it ring again, then puts down the paper and crosses to answer.

PAUL

Hello . .

SIDNEY

(*phone*) Hello . . it's me . .

PAUL

How are you . .

SIDNEY

Can I come up . .

PAUL

What do you mean . . where are you . .

245

SIDNEY
I'm outside in a booth . .

PAUL
Yeah sure . . come on up.

SIDNEY
How's Jonathan?

PAUL
He's not here. He recovered, I guess.

SIDNEY
He gave you quite a scare, didn't he.

PAUL
Yes. I've never seen him that drunk. He was really out cold.

SIDNEY
He was all right this morning?

PAUL
He bumped his head on the stairs, that's all. I'm sure he never felt it.
Come on up, we can talk in person.

SIDNEY
You sure you don't mind . .

PAUL
I said come up.

SIDNEY
Oh . . OK . . 'bye . .

PAUL
'Bye . . (*He hangs up . . ponders . . crosses to kitchen and makes
preparations for instant coffee. Water in pot . . light on . . pot on
stove. Knock on door. Paul goes to door and opens it. Sidney enters.*)

SIDNEY
Hi . .

PAUL
You look cold . . You've been in the booth all night?

SIDNEY
No . .

PAUL
Hmmmmm, sit down . . I'm making some coffee . . (*she does just
that, crosses and sits*) So . . what happened . .

SIDNEY
Nothing . .

PAUL

See . . I told you it wouldn't be so bad . . It always seems worse than it really is . .

SIDNEY

I didn't go home . .

PAUL

What???

SIDNEY

I didn't go home . .

PAUL

Where did you go???

SIDNEY

Well, I went home . . to the apartment . . but I didn't go in . .

PAUL

What the hell did you do that for . . Every cop in New York is going to be looking for you . . what's the matter with you.

SIDNEY

(*shrugs*) I don't know . .

PAUL

Here we go again . . What the hell happened . .

SIDNEY

I just went back to the building . . and I got in the elevator and went up to my floor . . and got out . . and went to the door and . . I didn't go in . .

PAUL

You stood there all night . .

SIDNEY

I just went back down . . and out again . .

PAUL

Where'd you sleep last night . . (*Sidney shrugs*) What does that mean . . Where did you sleep last night?

SIDNEY

(*shrugs*) Nowhere . .

PAUL

What do you mean nowhere . . you must have slept somewhere . .

SIDNEY

No . . I just . . no . .

PAUL

You just what . . You went outside after you went home and what . .

SIDNEY

I . . just walked around . . and . . I went down to Grand Central and read a pocket book . .

PAUL

All night . .

SIDNEY

Tess of the d'Urbervilles . .

PAUL

Good for you . . and then what . .

SIDNEY

I . . had breakfast . .

PAUL

What, coffee and a donut . .

SIDNEY

I don't know . .

PAUL

And . .

SIDNEY

I walked around . . I went to the library and fell asleep on the table next to an old man who was reading *Peter Rabbit* . . and . . I looked in windows . . and I had a hot dog . . and walked around . . and I called . . I called earlier but nobody was here . . about five.

PAUL

And you haven't slept . . or eaten, really.

SIDNEY

So?

PAUL

So? It's amazing the police haven't picked you up . . Your parents have no idea where you are . .

SIDNEY

No . .

PAUL

Fine . . you don't think they're worried . .

SIDNEY

I called them last night . .

PAUL

Yeah, you called them and said . . I'll be right home . . I'm all right . . I'll explain later . . and you disappear . . What's the matter with you?

SIDNEY

I don't know . . I told you I'm . .

PAUL

What . .

SIDNEY

Nothing . .

PAUL

Yeah . . you say it and I'll give you a good wallop . . well . . what are you going to do . .

SIDNEY

Can I stay . . here . . tonight . .

PAUL

Sidney . . For Christ's sake . . that's not the answer. You can stay here till kingdom come . . How about your parents? They don't know where you are . . Don't you think you ought to tell them . . You were supposed to be home at eleven o'clock *two nights ago.*

SIDNEY

I don't care . .

PAUL

You're not a child, for God's sake . . You've got to tell them . .

SIDNEY

Let the police pick me up . . I don't care . .

PAUL

Maybe you don't care . . but your parents care . .

SIDNEY

They probably don't care either . .

PAUL

Look, let's stop playing kindergarten . . and get you out of this mess . .

SIDNEY

Paul, can I stay here tonight, please . .

PAUL

Sidney . . You've got to tell them . .

SIDNEY

Can I please . .

PAUL

I'll call your father. (*goes to phone*)

SIDNEY

Paul . . please . .

PAUL

What is your number? Hello, operator . . Can I have the number of a

. . what's your last name? (*Sidney just sits*) Sidney . . Look . . (*hangs up*) You've got to tell the truth someday . . You can't walk around with all these things tied up in you . . Goddamnit, Sidney, we can't go through this every time . . I thought we decided about this!

SIDNEY

Can I stay here tonight?

PAUL

YES! . . NO! Ohhhhhhhhh. (*phone rings*) Where is Jonathan now? Hello . .

PETER

(*phone*) I'm coming up . .

PAUL

Why . .

PETER

I'm the big polite guy . . I called . . see you in a minute . . (*clicks off*)

PAUL

(*hanging up*) Peter . . He's coming . .

SIDNEY

Where's Jonathan . .

PAUL

Oh . . he said he was going to meet Father Wagoner for dinner, I think . . Maybe he'll be sober tonight . .

SIDNEY

We had a minister once who got drunk before his service . .

PAUL

Yeah?

SIDNEY

It was a funny sermon . . He was a very young minister and he didn't like it . . and he thought he could get out of it all this way . . That's what they said . .

PAUL

Did he get out of it . .

SIDNEY

I guess so . . He left . . I thought it was the best sermon all year . . He said everything about the church that should have been said for years . .

PAUL

And then he got out of it . .

SIDNEY

That's what they said . . (*Knock. Paul rises, opens door for Peter.*)

PETER

Hello, screwhead . . Well . . Hello, Sidney . . again . . Moving in?
. . Maybe I will too . . how about it . .

PAUL

Sure . . bring friends too . .

PETER

OK . . Where's the bishop?

PAUL

He's having dinner, I think . . with Father Wagoner . . I think that's
tonight . .

PETER

Yeah . . he was all set to take Rome . . Listen . . This girl you know
. . Prudy Primrose . . I swear to God that's her name . . She's the
girl I met in the hotel lobby, you know . . Well she's having a party
tomorrow night . . So if you want to come . . She said bring friends
. . you know . . It should be quite a thing . . she has many bucks this
girl . . So . .

PAUL

So . .

PETER

So come . . screwhead . . Live, love, and be happy . . Or are you going to sit here and brood . . Christ, if you want to fall into some girls
with money . . Just come a-long . .

PAUL

Well, let's see tomorrow night . . Give me a call then . .

PETER

What's with you . .

SIDNEY

Nothing . .

PETER

Your parents give you shit . .

SIDNEY

No . .

PETER

They didn't??? My ass . . what happened . .

PAUL

Guess . .

PETER

I don't know . . what happened . .

PAUL

She hasn't been home yet . .

PETER

Oh no . . Sidney baby . . when you step in it you step in it all the way
. . They're going to take you home in a paddy wagon . .

PAUL

I told her . .

PETER

Did she call . .

PAUL

Ask her.

PETER

Did you call?

SIDNEY

I called last night . . and said I'd be home . .

PETER

And you haven't been home . .

PAUL

She hasn't been to bed . . She read a book in Grand Central Station.

PETER

Christ, you gotta call . .

PAUL

We've been all through this, Peter . . She's got to call . . but . . what
she's going to say is a different matter . .

PETER

What the hell's the difference. Give 'em some bullshit . .

PAUL

She's got to tell them eventually.

PETER

She doesn't have to tell them anything . .

PAUL

Peter, you can't live forever not telling anybody what you're doing . .
They're going to find out sooner or later . . About her jobs . . about
everything . . This is killing her . .

PETER

What the hell do you care . . That's her problem . . You want to call
up and tell 'em she slept here Saturday . . go ahead . .

PAUL

We've got to call . .

PETER

I'll call . .

PAUL

Peter . .

PETER

(*at phone*) I said I'll call . . Ask Sidney . . Her parents love my ass . .

PAUL

Peter . .

PETER

Ask her . . (*dials*)

SIDNEY

If anybody can do it . .

PETER

Yeah . .

PAUL

Do what . . Do what . .

PETER

Thank you . . (*dials*) Hello . . Mr. Marchant . . This is Peter . . How are you, sir. Fine. Look, I don't want you to worry about your daughter. She's in good hands. It's just that . . ah . . I took her out to dinner last night . . and ah . . she ate something that didn't agree with her . . So I took her back to my home and had my own physician come and look at her and I think in the process we got confused as to who was going to call you and tell you. I know it may sound confusing, but . . in trying to take care of Sidney . . I thought I gave my physician orders to call you and tell you she was all right. Oh . . Oh . . last night? . . Yes, *this* was *Saturday* night. (*gives the two a weird look*) Ah . . last night she called? . . Yes . . She called and . . but I checked with my physician and he said she'd better not go out . . She was weak . . you see we had to pump her stomach . . It was some rotten oysters or something . . But she's in good hands . . I would have called if I had known . . I'll ah . . I'll speak to my doctor about that . . Oh . . She's fine . . (*Sidney shakes her head "No"*) Yes . . she'll be home tonight . . Yes . . Fine . . No, no. I'll bring her . . Fine . . good night. (*hangs up*) Well, they said it couldn't be done.

PAUL

And you did it. Now we have a stomach pump story to add to the fire.

SIDNEY

I'm not going . .

PAUL

Oh yes you are . . It's showdown time all over the world.

PETER

I told you he loved my ass . . Just go home . . and look a little sick
. . My imaginary doctor just took the rap . .

PAUL

Anybody ever tell you you're a genius . .

PETER

Ahhhhhhh yes . . Once . . an eighteen-year-old Spic from Rochester
. . she . .

PAUL

Come on . . Jesus . . turn him on . . and . . pfffffft . . (*noise at
the door, key in the lock*) This is Jonathan . . (*door opens — this is
Jonathan*) back from the wars . .

JONATHAN

The Crusades, my sons, the Crusades! Sidney . . (*he goes to her and
they have a hello embrace*) How did you ever get out.

PAUL

Here we go again. On good behavior . .

JONATHAN

You're going to get sick again . . if you don't watch out . .

PETER

Or the big bad wolf will eat her up . .

JONATHAN

Hmmmm. (*taking off his coat and dropping it on chair*)

PAUL

Hang it, Jonathan . .

JONATHAN

Oh yes, oh yes . . never learn . . (*takes it to closet*)

PAUL

How are you, Jonathan . .

JONATHAN

Well, I thought all day Sunday I'd never be the same . . but you are a
wonderful team of surgeons . . Do you know what it was . . do you
know what it was . .

PAUL

You told us . .

JONATHAN

Yes . . well this insane man . . kept insisting that I drink to a free Ireland . . I always thought Ireland was free . . but . . at any rate . . the liquor was . . I still have a bump.

PAUL

Yes, I noticed your head marks on the stairs . .

PETER

Shit, Jonathan, you scared the pants off old screwhead here . .

JONATHAN

Oh . . old Jonathan never dies . . He's just been fading for twenty-eight years . . Well look . . I'm almost sober . . tonight . . eh . . I couldn't resist . . Father Wagoner bought me a few drinks . .

PAUL

Well, you met Father Wagoner . .

JONATHAN

Met him . . Let me tell you . . Let me tell you . . this is a fantastic man . . This is a fantastic man . . Yes I met him and this is a fantastic man . . and we talked about everything . . and do you know . . before I came back I stood in the church for almost an hour by myself . . This . . really was something . . I want to tell you . . (*going to bar*)

PAUL

Watch it, Jonathan . .

JONATHAN

Yes . . yes . . (*pouring some Scotch*)

PETER

Jonathan . . I've got a great assed party I want you to go to . . this Prudy Primrose . . Tomorrow night . . Let me tell you . .

JONATHAN

Let me tell you . . this is a fantastic man . . I want to tell you that . . I stood in that church for one hour . . after I talked to that man . . for one hour . . and let me tell you . . I think that I have a calling . .

PAUL

Oh shit, Jonathan . .

JONATHAN

I think that I have a calling . .

PAUL

All right today it's to the cloth . .

JONATHAN

Today . . and tomorrow . . and to the cloth . . it was something . .

PETER

Jonathan . . How about this party . . You remember Prudy Primrose . .

JONATHAN

We talked . . Father Wagoner and I talked for I don't know how long and he told me about when he first went to seminary . . and his first church . . and his congregation . . and his problems . . and . . and . . this man has led such a vast . . such a vast life . . He has traveled . . you know he has traveled . . and he has dealt with people . . that . . You know . . what I mean . . you know . . and . . he is . . he is just so filled . . so fulfilled. It's just something I . . I felt . . I felt . . there is accomplishment . . there . .

PAUL

Well, we have all the makings here of a spiritual revival . . Jonathan, where would you like your church built . . We have all the necessities . . We have a sinner . . Do we have a sinner?

PETER

We have Peter, Paul, and Jon . . what else do we need?

PAUL

There you go . . Peter, Paul, and Jon . . The disciples are traveling the weary road at night and they come upon a lovely young miss . . not yet converted to the cause . .

JONATHAN

Sidney . . Sidney . . Sidney . . Do you know . . what a time . .

PAUL

Well, Peter. Well, Jonathan . . what do we do . . with this young miss . .

PETER

What do you think, Paul . .

PAUL

Is she a Christian or not . .

JONATHAN

Is she a Christian? She's a Sidney . .

PETER

We don't know her name, shithead . . we just met her . .

PAUL

We ask her name . . Ask her name, Disciple . .

JONATHAN

What is your name . . (*she is embarrassed by the game, shrugs*)

PAUL

She doesn't know her name . . What shall we call her . .

PETER

How about Levine!

JONATHAN

Levine? How is he? You have . .

PAUL

Call her Levine. And what is she doing . .

PETER

She's sitting in the road waiting for the apostles to tell her about Christ . . for Christ's sake . .

PAUL

She's sitting in the road, Jonathan . . show her the light . .

JONATHAN

My dear . . see the light . .

PAUL

You'll have to do better than that, Jonathan . . be persuasive.

PETER

Sell her an encyclopedia.

JONATHAN

Wouldn't you like to be a Christian?

SIDNEY

I . . don't know . .

PAUL

Tell her all the advantages . .

JONATHAN

Well . . you'll be one of the majority . . if you dislike prejudice . .

PAUL

This is almost two thousand years ago . .

JONATHAN

Well . . you'll be in the minority if you don't like . . ah . . crowds . .

PAUL

And can we not cleanse her of her sins . .

PETER

Watch yourself, boys . .

JONATHAN

Of course . . of course . . What are your sins, my dear girl.

SIDNEY

I don't know . .

257

JONATHAN

She doesn't know . .

PAUL

Well, that's a sin right there . .

JONATHAN

It is?

PAUL

Why not . .

JONATHAN

All right . . We will cleanse you and make you a follower of Christ . . and you will reap the benefits . . reap the benefits . . right? And if you are a good girl . . we will canonize you . . and you will never be forgotten . . You will be St. Sidney . . St. Sidney . . now doesn't that sound wonderful . .

SIDNEY

Yes . .

JONATHAN

Certainly . .

PAUL

That's it, Jonathan . . you're in form . .

PETER

You screwoffs . .

JONATHAN

Certainly . . then rise forth, Sidney . . and join us in our march . . for we will convert the world to our cause . .

PETER

Give her the secret grip, Jonathan . .

JONATHAN

The grip . . the grip . . is a kiss. (*kisses her on the cheek*)

PAUL

And the song . .

JONATHAN

And the song . .

> Jon, Jon the grey ghost is gone . .
> And it must be a very fine town oh.

And now???

PAUL

We all give her the grip . .

PETER

I'll buy that . .

PAUL

Easy, Disciple . . easy . . (*Paul kisses her on cheeks, then Peter*)

SIDNEY

That's the nicest kiss you ever gave me, Peter . .

PAUL

You see . . she's one of us . .

JONATHAN

She's free . . Hoho . . Now . . Now what . .

PAUL

Pronounce her something . .

JONATHAN

What?

PAUL

Well she's a Christian now . . pronounce her that . .

JONATHAN

They didn't do it that way . .

PAUL

Well, they certainly didn't do it this way . .

JONATHAN

I pronounce you St. Sidney . .

PAUL

Not yet. Jonathan . . not yet . .

JONATHAN

Why not? Let it be done . . I pronounce you St. Sidney . . hail.

PETER AND PAUL

Hail . . (*a sudden silence as music plays — the record ends*)

PETER

Well that's enough of this crap . .

PAUL

(*turns phonograph off*) Well done . .

SIDNEY

You're all silly . .

JONATHAN

Yes . . my dear . . But would we could do it . . I tell you . . I tell you . .

PETER

Here we go . .

PAUL

Jonathan . . is it going to mean a job . .

JONATHAN

Oh . . Ohh. I . . I have to call Father Wagoner tomorrow morning . . now . . You wake me when you leave for work . . when you leave . . tomorrow . . You wake me . .

PAUL

Yeah . . I'll wake you . . And I think Sidney here ought to go home now . . while it's early . .

SIDNEY

I'm not going to go . .

PAUL

You've got to go, Sidney . . You've got to go sometime . .

SIDNEY

No, I don't . .

JONATHAN

What's the matter?

PAUL

She doesn't want to face her parents . .

JONATHAN

For what . . What did you do . . my dear . .

PETER

For screwing round when she was supposed to be home . .

JONATHAN

Just because you stay with us you're not going to get sick again . . I'll tell them . . I'll tell them that . .

PAUL

She's got to go home, Jonathan . .

JONATHAN

Let her stay awhile . .

PAUL

Awhile . . then awhile longer, and then what . . Look, you have to go home . . I'll . . take you home . .

SIDNEY

I don't care . . I'm not going . .

PAUL

For Christ's sake, Sidney . . you can't stay here forever . . Some day you've got to tell your parents what is going on . . You've got to tell them . .

PETER

Why don't you leave her alone . . I'll take her home . .

PAUL

That's fine . . and you can make up another story . .

PETER

What the hell's she going to tell them . . They don't listen to her anyway.

PAUL

But they listen to you . . they listen to you . . that's funny . . Maybe because you talk so much . .

PETER

I'll take care of her . .

PAUL

She'll take care of herself . .

SIDNEY

Jonathan, I want to stay . .

JONATHAN

It's all right, my dear . .

PAUL

It's not all right, Jonathan . . She's worked her problem from little insignificant happenings into one great big mess. If you had told your parents when you quit your first job . . you would have been all right . . now you have another and you quit that . . and you'll go on and on and on . . making up more and more stories . . getting more and more screwed up till they carry you away . . all because of one stupid little thing . .

SIDNEY

That's right, I'm crazy.

PAUL

That's right, you're crazy then . . You can be anything that makes it easier for you . . You can stay here forever . . You can keep putting it off with your parents . .

PETER

Her parents don't know what the hell's coming off; they don't understand her . .

PAUL

Do you understand her??? How the hell can they understand her. She probably doesn't tell them anything . . She probably sits around like she does here . . and says I don't know . . and shrugs . . and moans . . and gets pushed whatever way they want to push her . . They probably don't know what she wants . . What would you think if your daugh-

261

ter came home from school . . five months pregnant with a girdle strapped around her to try to keep it in . . like nothing had happened . .

SIDNEY

Paul . . please . . I . . Jonathan . .

PAUL

Wouldn't you think you'd been left out of something . . wouldn't you think your daughter would break it to you early enough so that she could be taken care of properly?

JONATHAN

Why are you doing this?

SIDNEY

Paul . .

PAUL

So that she wouldn't have to go around with a great peck of elastic around her stomach trying to get her way through a semester at school . . when she knew damn well . . damn well . . sooner or later she had to have the baby . . They had to find out . .

SIDNEY

Paul . . (*now in tears*) Jonathan . . doesn't know . . Oh Christ . . Paul (*runs, crying wildly, into the bathroom*) Jonathan . . Jonathan . .

JONATHAN

Why did you have to say this??? Why did you, did you say this???

PAUL

Let's finish this, Jonathan . .

PETER

For Christ's sake . . she didn't want him to know . .

JONATHAN

You didn't have to tell me . . while she was here . . Why did you . .

PAUL

I'm sorry . . I'm sorry . . She doesn't want anybody to know . . She wraps herself all up in those goddamn little things until they grab her like that goddamn girdle . . until they really do become something . . God knows how many thousands of little things she could blow if she wanted to let go . . For Christ's sake . . she's a lovely young woman . . why the hell keep her screwed up with tall stories . .

PETER

You didn't have to tell Jonathan . . That's one person she wanted to keep from it . . You are an ass, you know that . . You're a real screw-head . .

262

JONATHAN

Please . . Let's not say any more . .

PAUL

Goddamnit, Jonathan, let's finish this . . That girl is going home tonight
. . and she's going to start from the top and she's going to lay it straight
to them . . If she wants to go back to school . . she's got to lay it
straight to them . .

JONATHAN

(*looks at his hands*) It's the rash . . It's coming back . . the rash . .

PETER

Shall we make up a list of everyone she's slept with . .

PAUL

Let's do that, friend, let's do that . . At least she has some convictions
about screwing, doesn't she . . At least she makes a choice, doesn't she
. . At least she sleeps with somebody she wants to . .

JONATHAN

THE RASH . .

PETER

Won't mom love that . .

PAUL

Well, it pisses *you* off . .

PETER

I couldn't give a shit . . but her old man . .

PAUL

Her old man's gonna find out . . For's God's sake, Peter . . If she
can't help it . . then she needs a doctor . . If she just wants to . .
that's that . . then she's got to tell him that . . and *he's* got to help her.

JONATHAN

Look at my hands . . we've got to stop . .

PETER

What do you think they've kept her in . . for . .

PAUL

And didn't it help . . my, didn't it help . . Has she ever told them how
she feels about sex . . how she feels about working, how she feels about
going back to school . .

PETER

How the hell should I know . .

JONATHAN

MY RASH IS COMING BACK . . WE . .

PAUL

Hell, I sweated here the other night trying to find out how she felt about anything . . And I'm not her father . .

JONATHAN

Haven't we said enough. HAVEN'T WE SAID ENOUGH??? Now I have something; I want to read you something . . from the missal . . that I remembered . . that we talked about today . . *I* have something . .

PAUL

Look, Jonathan, I'm sorry . . She didn't want you to know . .

JONATHAN

Well, let's . . just . . just . . listen . . I have something . . (*looks at his hands*) to say . . to say . .

PAUL

Let's get her out of the bathroom . .

JONATHAN

I want her to hear it too . .

PAUL

(*crossing to door*) Sidney . . Come on out of there . . Sidney . . Jonathan knows now you didn't have rheumatic fever . . I know you didn't have rheumatic fever . . Peter knows . . the whole goddamn world knows . . Now come on out of there . . you've got a lot of other things to get off your chest . . Now come out of there . . and let me take you home . .

JONATHAN

I wonder if she has it too . .

PETER

She's probably hanging in the shower.

PAUL

You're very funny . .

JONATHAN

Sidney . . Sidney . . come out . . I want to tell you about this afternoon . . I want everybody to hear . . I want you to hear . .

SIDNEY

(*from inside*) Jonathan . . I'm sorry . . Jonathan . .

JONATHAN

Sidney . . come out . . come out . . it's all right . .

SIDNEY

I can't, Jonathan . . I'm sorry . .

PAUL

We know that, Sidney . . Now come out and see the world . . for God's sake . .

SIDNEY

I can't . .

JONATHAN

Sidney . . it's all right . . It's all right . . Sidney . . can you hear me . . Sidney, can you hear me . .

SIDNEY

Yes . .

JONATHAN

Sidney . . It's all right . . *I knew about it before* . . I already knew . . so it doesn't matter . . You see it doesn't matter . . it's all right . . please come out . . we still love you . .

PAUL

Sonofabitch. (*door opens; Sidney stands there*)

JONATHAN

It's all right . . I knew . .

PAUL

Come on kiddo . . let's go . . (*holds out his hand*)

SIDNEY

Ohhhhhhhhhh. (*She runs into Jonathan's arms and cries. Paul throws off the hand she refused and walks away.*)

JONATHAN

It's all right . . it's all right . .

PAUL

It's fine, Jonathan . . but let's get her to stop crying . . and start home . . We can all go . . It'll do us some good . . How about it . .

JONATHAN

Yes yes . . but . . I want to tell you what happened today . .

PAUL

We know what happened . . You had dinner with Father Wagoner.

JONATHAN

No no no . . I mean after that . . after . . It was miraculous . . It really was . .

PETER

Somebody bought you a bar, Jonathan . .

JONATHAN

No . . I mean it . . I really mean it . . Peter . . I really mean it . .

LEE H. KALCHEIM

PETER

Jonathan, do you really mean it?

JONATHAN

I really mean it . . something miraculous happened . .

PAUL

Jonathan saw God!!!

JONATHAN

Now you don't want to listen to me . .

PETER

We want to listen to you . .

PAUL

Jonathan . .

JONATHAN

You don't want to listen . . but I'm going to tell you . .

PAUL

Tell us, Jonathan . . Tell us please . . tell us . .

JONATHAN

I *will* tell you, Peter . . are you listening . . Paul . .

PAUL AND PETER

Yes . . yes . . Jonathan . .

JONATHAN

Sidney . . Do you know what happened after I had dinner . . (*she nods*) Well . . you see . . you see, after Father Wagoner and I had dinner . . he took me back to the church . . He took me back to the church and showed me the whole place . . It's a lovely church. He showed me everything . . and gave me some of the history . . and told me stories about himself . . and the church . . and we talked about me . . and about what I wanted to do . . and when you talk to this man you feel like you are accomplishing something . . that . . that a conversation with this man is . . is a catharsis in itself . . No, I mean . . that . . I mean that . . And so when we were finished and he told me to call him tomorrow . . I walked from his office back into the church . . and I stood. You see I stood, just stood in the nave . . and looked down the aisle . . at the cross . . and I felt so peculiar suddenly . . as if this was a very important moment . . You get that feeling sometimes . . you get that feeling . . and I stood in the nave and, maybe it was . . just the Gothic weight of the church itself pressing on me . . Or just the silence . . Or just strange solemnity that I always find in churches, but I began hearing . . I began hearing things . . sounds . . and voices . . recollections . . and I heard a chorus singing . . No I did . . I

266

have heard choruses before . . but I heard them singing hallelujahs . .
And suddenly for no reason at all I thought of my brother . . I thought
of Michael . . and I thought of Michael . . and I heard him chuckle
. . the way he would chuckle when he found something new for his junk
pile . . The way he chuckled when he found the ball from an old brass
bedstead . . and told my fortune in it . . the way he chuckled . . and
I stood in the nave . . and I shouted all the way down the aisle . . I
shouted so the cross would hear me . . I shouted . . Hellooooo,
Michael . . Hellooooo . . and he chuckled and I could hear him smile
. . yes I could hear him smile . . and then I could hear my father telling me . . that . . telling me that Michael had had an accident . . that
Michael had had an accident . . and hung himself by mistake and that
I should never play with rope . . that it was very dangerous . . and I
said yes to my father but I knew . . I knew what had happened . . because I knew Michael very well . . and Michael never had an accident
. . whatever happened to Michael was his own doing . . and when
Michael did something well he succeeded . . and when he failed . . he
would suffer . . and that's the word, suffer . . you see – you see . .
suffer . . Just not having neat handwriting . . suffer . . And I said,
Michael, hellooooo . . Michael . . tell me . . Why did you do it . .
I didn't expect an answer really . . I didn't expect anything but my
echo . . I was still hearing the echo from Hellooooo, Michael . . But
I asked him and he said . . what I knew he would say . . He said just
that . . he said . . because I am ashamed . . because I am ashamed,
and it feels terrible . . and I'm afraid it will happen again and again the
longer I live . . and all you get for it is sympathy . . and sympathy is
not the cure . . the only cure is strength . . the only cure is strength
. . I heard him say that to me . . and that's a nine-year-old boy . .
and that was a nine-year-old boy . . a nine-year-old man . . who refused to feel like that again . . And I said . . Hellooooo, Michael . .
Hello . . I said . . are you in heaven or hell . . where are you . . and
he said . . I'm in neither . . I'm in purgatory . . I'm still waiting to
be judged. He's still waiting to be judged you see . . He said . . I committed a crime . . because I murdered . . but they think I may not be
responsible for my crime . . now isn't that silly. I hung myself and I'm
not responsible . . that is very silly . . and I don't like it here. I don't
like it here . . and I must be delivered . . You must come to God . .
and deliver me . . he said . . that . . he said, Deliver me, Jonathan
. . So . . I must you see. I have a calling. I stood in the nave and I
have a calling. I can deliver him . . I can . . He asked *me* for . . he

asked me . . he said . . I don't like it here . . I don't like it here . .
I don't like it . . here . . deliver me . . please . . (*they stand as
Jonathan relaxes*)

PAUL

Well, Jonathan's going to be Pope.

PETER

That's very funny . .

PAUL

You're amused, aren't you . .

PETER

I thought that was very funny . .

PAUL

You think the whole thing is very funny. Let's all chuckle to ourselves
while Jonathan makes a living ass of himself . .

PETER

For Christ's sake . . you can see he cares about this thing . .

PAUL

What for now . . for now . . as if you won't walk out of here and have
a new Jonathan story to throw around . . No one thinks it's funnier
than you do . .

PETER

What's the matter with you, for God's sake . .

PAUL

Nothing . . I'm just tired of you laughing out of the side of your mouth
while Jonathan makes an ass of himself . .

PETER

Maybe he means this, maybe he means this . .

PAUL

Jonathan knows damn well when he wakes up tomorrow morning he
won't remember a goddamn thing . . He'll no more want to be Father
Jonathan . . than some other half-assed thing . .

JONATHAN

No no no no no no . . this is very important . . I told you this is very
significant . . I'm not going to forget . .

PAUL

And you weren't going to forget the book of poems that you were going
to wake up and write the next day . . and you weren't going to forget
the boat you were going to take to Italy . . and you weren't going to
forget the play you were going to read for . . and you weren't going
to forget to sign up at NYU and get your degree and teach . . and teach

. . and every morning . . the alarm just doesn't go off . . and every morning . . we greet the sober world with a smile . . and commit all our ambitions to memories . . Next time you hear a calling . . don't tell anybody about it, Jonathan . . just go . . just go . . and write from where you are . . then I'll believe you . . Jonathan, for God's sake, Father Wagoner just wants you to run his damn mimeograph machine. He just wants you to print up the church quarterly. Where the hell do you get these ideas?

JONATHAN

He told me to call him tomorrow.

PAUL

That's right. Are you going to forget? *Call him. He's* got the calling, Jonathan. Not you!!!

JONATHAN

Don't tell me, Paul. I heard the voice. I was there you know, you weren't there.

PAUL

I'm sure you were there. I'm sure you were all there.

JONATHAN

But you don't understand. This is not the same. This is not the same.

PAUL

Please, Jonathan.

PETER

Why don't you listen to him. For God's sake, he's here so listen to him.

JONATHAN

Yes yes yes yes. LISTEN TO ME!!! (*jumps up on chair*) Listen to me. I want to show you . . I want to show you . . (*takes out of his pocket a missal*) You see this. This is my missal. Father Wagoner gave it to me . . And inside I have a list with the times for my classes . . my meetings.

PAUL

Your meetings?

JONATHAN

My meetings with Father Wagoner . . You see, I may run the mimeo — mimeo whatever it is . . but I will be paid for that . . and I will pay my rent with that . . and I will be instructed for that, by the indestructible Father Wagoner who has great respect for my oratorical ability, for my brain, and for my future as a man of the cloth. Me. Jonathan J Man-of-the-Cloth.

PAUL

Let me see that.

JONATHAN

No no . . *noli me tangere* . .

PAUL

Let me see it . .

JONATHAN

No no . . that's my private book . . for appointments with God . .

PAUL

That's lovely, Jonathan . . let me see it . .

PETER

What do you want to see it for . .

PAUL

'Cause I think it's a lot of shit . .

PETER

You don't believe anything he says . .

PAUL

Do you? Let me see it . . (*He lunges for it. Jonathan jumps down and backs away with it.*) Let me see it, Jonathan . .

JONATHAN

No . . no . . I want to keep it . . It's my meetings with Father Wagoner . . I can't lose this . . because I can't forget the meetings . . You see. I'm going to be someone . . You see we can both be someone . .

PAUL

Just let me see it . .

JONATHAN

When I be someone . . you see . .

PAUL

Come on, Jonathan, stop playing games . .

JONATHAN

(*they are still pacing, Paul stalking Jonathan, Jonathan backing away*) I'm not playing . . (*suddenly Paul goes after him and a merry chase goes . . they really run, in, out, around chairs, in and around the kitchen table, while Peter and Sidney stand back not knowing quite how to take the whole thing*)

PAUL

Come on, Jonathan, give me that goddamn thing . .

JONATHAN

It's my sacred tablet . .

PAUL

Will you stop fooling with yourself . . and let me see that . . I don't believe a damn word you say . . now . . let . . me . . (*they chase back into the living room area; finally Paul lunges for Jonathan and they go on the floor*)

JONATHAN

No no no no no no no . . don't . . No no . . don't!!! (*And Paul breaks away . . with the book. Out of breath he flips the pages. Jonathan rises slowly.*)

PETER

Have a good run, boys . .

JONATHAN

(*holds out hand*) Please . .

PAUL

What's this? (*holds book to Jonathan*)

JONATHAN

That's every Tuesday and Thursday . . one to four . . my meetings . . that's his handwriting . . (*Paul looks at the book. Jonathan holds out his hand.*) Please . . (*Paul looks at the book*) I've got a surprise for you, Paul —

PAUL

What's that . .

JONATHAN

I'll tell you . . if you give me back the book . .

PAUL

What's your surprise, Jonathan . .

JONATHAN

If you'll give me back the book . .

PAUL

I'm going to give you back the book anyway . . What's your surprise . . Who did you meet . . what did you hear?

JONATHAN

I have a surprise . .

PETER

Hey, Jonathan . . are we going to run around again . . What is it?

JONATHAN

My poem is published. I have a poem published.

PAUL

What?

271

JONATHAN

One of my poems is published.

PETER

Where . .

PAUL

Yeah, where . .

JONATHAN

In a very respected publication . . Even I was surprised . .

PAUL

What respected publication . . *Harper's, New Yorker, Atlantic* . .

JONATHAN

That's right . .

PAUL

What's right . . the *Atlantic* . .

JONATHAN

Yes. I'm thinking very seriously of not even cashing the check . . I'm thinking very seriously of framing it.

PETER

When did all this happen?

JONATHAN

I told you it was a surprise . .

PAUL

You got one of *your* poems published in the *Atlantic*?

JONATHAN

That's my surprise . .

PAUL

I'll be goddamned . . I don't believe . . it . .

PETER

What the hell, he said he got the check . .

JONATHAN

I am going to be a famous poet . . I think we should all drink to that . . Sidney, would you like to drink to that . .

SIDNEY

Did you really get a poem published?

JONATHAN

Yes, I really did . .

PETER

(*begins laughing to himself*) OK . . Jonathan, let's toast our poet . .

JONATHAN

Yes . . Let me pour the drinks . . (*pours Scotch and puts some in glasses*) A very important toast . .

PAUL

When's it coming out, Jonathan . . when can we see it . .

JONATHAN

Oh, it's out this month . .

PAUL

This month???

PETER

Hehehe hehehe hehehe hehehe . .

PAUL

What are you laughing at??? This month . . Don't you have a copy?

JONATHAN

Yes . . And I'll show it to you after we toast . . and after you give me my book please . .

PAUL

(*notices he still has it*) Oh . . After I see it . . I'll . .

JONATHAN

Drinks . . everyone . . Sidney . . Peter . . Paul . .

PETER

Hehehe hehehe . .

PAUL

What is so funny with you?

PETER

Nothing . . noth– hehehe heheheh hehehe –ing . .

JONATHAN

Shall we toast . .

PETER

Yeah . . To . . hehehe . . to the new rising young poet . . Jonathan Dill . . hehehe . .

SIDNEY

Peter . . what's so . . funny . .

PETER

Drink . . drink . . to the new poet . . hear, hear . .

ALL

Hear hear . . (*they drink*)

PETER

(*cannot control himself*) Hehehe hehehe . .

PAUL

Why don't you let us in on it? What'd you do, take some kind of laughing gas . .

PETER

No . . hehehe . . I . . just think it's so funny . . It's so funny . . You should see yourself . .

PAUL

What's wrong with me . .

PETER

I think it's so funny . . Paulsie baby works his balls off working . . writing . . pushing . . and Jonathan . . just walks out and gets his poem published . . Hehehe hehehe hehehe . . I think that's funny . .

PAUL

What's funny about that . .

PETER

I'm sure you don't think it's funny . . hehehe . . Don't you think it's funny . . Jonathan . .

JONATHAN

I think . . that this marks a new era . . I really think . . that now I am going to be someone . . That Paul and I are going to be someone together . . right. Isn't that right, Paul . . That you are going to be someone with me . .

PAUL

What the hell are you talking about???

PETER

Hehehe hehehe hehehe hehehe hehehe.

PAUL

Will you shut up!!!

PETER

I think it's funny . . hehehe.

SIDNEY

You didn't tell me about this, Jonathan . .

PAUL

Let's see the poem . . I want to see the poem . .

PETER

What's the matter, don't you believe him . .

PAUL

I believe him . . I want to see it . . Don't you want to see it . .

PETER

I don't care . . I think it's funny, hehehe . .

PAUL

Yes, we know that . .

JONATHAN

Let's drink now a toast to Sidney . . to our new saint . .

PAUL

Let's see the poem . . Jonathan . . where is it . .

JONATHAN

I have it . . I have it . . Put my missal down first . . I want that . .
That's my regular job you see . . I don't know how many more poems
I will publish . . but that's my regular job . .

PETER

Hehehe . . You should look at yourself, Paulsie baby . . you look like
someone dropped a bomb on you . . hehehe . . You look like you just
flunked an exam . . a crucial exam . . hehehe hehehe . . Oh . .

PAUL

OK, laughing boy . . It's funny . . hah hah . . Here, Jonathan . .
Here's the missal . . (*holds it out*) Where's the poem . .

JONATHAN

In the closet . . in my coat . . in my pocket . .

SIDNEY

He didn't tell you anything about this before?

PAUL

No . . (*Jonathan goes to closet, opens it, goes into coat pocket, comes
out with a paper bag, comes back across the room holding the bag*)
What's that . .

JONATHAN

The poem . .

PAUL

What's it in a bag for . .

JONATHAN

I have more than one copy . .

PETER

He probably bought out the newsstand . . hehehe . .

PAUL

Let me see . . Let me see . .

JONATHAN

All right . . (*slowly pulls the paper off and holds out a pack of clean
white paper*)

PAUL

What's that . . (*leans in and looks*) For Christ's sake . . For Christ's

275

sake, Jonathan . . hahahhhh ahahahaha . . (*knocks the papers sky high — in a flurry they fly all over the room*)

PETER

What is it?

SIDNEY

What'd he do . .

PAUL

For Christ's sake, Jonathan . . YOU RAN THE POEMS OFF ON THE MIME-OGRAPH MACHINE. THOSE ARE MIMEOGRAPHED . . AHAHAHAHAHAHAH.

JONATHAN

They're published . . Give me the book . . It's the same thing.

PETER

Give him his book, you said you would . . (*Paul is now convulsed with laughter as Jonathan pursues him for the book*)

JONATHAN

They're published. Give me the missal. (*they stalk as Paul laughs and laughs*)

SIDNEY

What's so funny . . Why's he laughing.

PETER

I think he's happy . .

SIDNEY

Paul, don't play . . What are you laughing at . . Why is everyone laughing.

PAUL

I thought . . hehehe . . he had his poem published . . hehehe . . That's funny . . It's only mimeographed . . It's only . . mimeographed . . hehehe. I've had my opera photostated. Is that published too? huh? hehehe . .

JONATHAN

Paul . . Paul, what's funny. What are you laughing at . .

PAUL

Hehehe ha ha ha ha ha ha ha ha ha ha . .

PETER

Tell 'em what you're laughing at, Paulsie . .

PAUL

He he he he hahahahahah . .

JONATHAN

Paul . . what . . is it . .

SIDNEY

What's wrong with him?

PETER

Tell 'em, Paulsie . . tell 'em why you're so tickled . .

JONATHAN

Paul . .

PAUL

Ha ha ha ha ha ha ha ha . .

PETER

(*grabs him roughly*) Hey, shithead! Tell him!!!

PAUL

What . . tell him what . .

PETER

What's so funny . .

PAUL

(*takes paper*) That . . that's funny . .

PETER

That's not funny. You're funny. You don't know what you're laughing
at . .

PAUL

This . . I think it's funny . . this . .

PETER

(*grabs paper*) Tell him . . Tell him, screwoff!!!

PAUL

Who . . what . . Tell who . . what?

PETER

Why. You. Laugh.

PAUL

What's wrong with you?

PETER

What's wrong with you. You think it's amusing . . huh?

PAUL

What is this . . a joke . . what . . Jonathan, what is this?

JONATHAN

What is this, Peter?

PETER

What is this, Paulsie?

PAUL

All right now!!!

PETER
All right now!!!

PAUL
What's the matter with you?

PETER
What is the matter with *you*. Let me ask you something, Paulsie. What is
Jonathan doing here? What is he doing here?

JONATHAN
Well, I just came for . .

PETER
Not you . .

PAUL
You know. He came to get a job. Why . .

PETER
And . .

PAUL
And what . .

PETER
And what happened.

PAUL
He never got one . .

PETER
And . .

PAUL
And what?

PETER
And he stays . .

PAUL
Yeah . . he stays . .

PETER
And he looks, and he never makes it . .

PAUL
Not yet . .

PETER
And he never makes it.

PAUL
Yeah?

PETER
And St. Paul sits on his throne and says: Jonathan pick up your pants,
Jonathan do it yourself, Jonathan get up on time, Jonathan get the job.

Get that job . . block that kick . . But through it all Jonathan stays . . and stays and stays and stays . . Until one day . . you come home from work. (*goes to pile of records and picks them up*) You come home and say to Jonathan . . (*goes to Jonathan*) "Guess what, Jonathan, I've sold my opera . . and it's been recorded . . and millions of people want to buy it . . Here . . free records just for you . . (*putting pile of records on*) Here . . listen . . (*the record drops and rock and roll instrumental blares*) Listen . . Jonathan . . I'm a success . . (*going back to Jonathan*) I'm a success now, Jonathan, and I don't need you anymore. (*takes suitcase and puts it on floor by Jonathan*) Here . . Thanks for staying on!!! (*the music continues under and fades*)

PAUL

Who needs who, for Christ's sake.

PETER

You need him, buddy boy . . 'cause he makes you look good!!!

PAUL

You sonofabitch you . .

PETER

Next to failure . . anything looks good.

PAUL

You sonofabitch.

PETER

That's right. That's what I am. Peter J. Sonofabitch. And everybody knows it. Everybody knows it . . but one . . one . . not one goddamn person knows who you are . . No one except maybe I do . . now!

JONATHAN

Can't we stop this. We're all friends. Why are you doing this?

PETER

Because you'll be here forever, Jonathan . . Who's helping who?

PAUL

What do you want me to do, for God's sake. Kick him down the stairs???

PETER

YES . . YES YES YES YES YES YES. Kick him down the stairs . . Get him out of here . .

PAUL

So he can go drinking with you.

PETER

That's not your problem . . He doesn't belong in this city . . you know that . . how long did it take you to find that out . . Does it take

279

months to find out . . that it won't work . . Kick him down the stairs
. . Yes . . and then you tell me you don't miss him . . You tell me *that*.

JONATHAN

Peter . . please . . Look I want to finish . .

PETER

Tell me you wouldn't miss him . .

PAUL

Tell you this and tell you that. Who the hell are you???

PETER

No, friend . . that's my question . . who the hell are *you* . .

PAUL

You're crazy . .

PETER

Some day when Jonathan's gone . . you tell me . . huh . . you tell
me the truth . .

PAUL

You're goddamn crazy . .

JONATHAN

Look please . . please . . We're all going to break out in a minute . .
Look at my hands . . something's wrong . . you see something's
wrong . . but I know . . I heard . . today . . we can be saved . .
like Michael . . we can but . .

SIDNEY

Jonathan, I don't feel well . .

JONATHAN

Everything will be all right, my dear . . Let me show you . . You see
. . Here is the altar . . (*runs to the stuffed chair and turns it around*)

PETER

OK, let him run . . let him run . .

PAUL

Jonathan, please . .

JONATHAN

I want to show you all . . (*has come from kitchen with large spoons
he hands each of them*) Now hold your crosses up . . (*climbs on the
chair and opens his missal*)

SIDNEY

(*crosses to chair and sits on the arm, looking to Jonathan*) Jonathan . .
take me home . .

PAUL

Jonathan, all right, we get the point . .

PETER

I think we're part of something . . (*holds his spoon*)

JONATHAN

I have a prayer . . I have a prayer . . I found after I was called . . now . . I will read . . It is important because things have changed . . things *have* changed.

PAUL

Jonathan . .

PETER

Amen.

PAUL

God . . (*frustrated, he turns on the scene*)

JONATHAN

Brethren, understand for it is now the hour for us to rise from sleep, because now our salvation is nearer than when we came to believe. The night is far advanced; the day is at hand. Let us therefore lay aside the works of darkness and put on the armor of light. Let us walk becomingly as in the day, not in revelry and drunkenness, not in debauchery and wantonness, not in strife and jealousy, but put on the Lord, Jesus Christ. Thanks be to God . .

SIDNEY

(*begins to cry again*) Jonathan . . take me home . . please . .

JONATHAN

"None of them that wait on Theee shall be confounded . ."

PAUL

Jonathan, all right!!!

PETER

Do something Paul . . huh? Do something. Who the hell are you?

JONATHAN

"Oh Lord, Show O Lord Thy ways to me and teach me Thy paths."

PAUL

Peter, shuddup!!!

JONATHAN

Oh Lord . .

PAUL

Jonathan, shuddup. Everybody. Just shut up . .

JONATHAN

"Show, oh Lord, Thy ways to me and teach me Thy paths . ."

PAUL

What the hell is going on here? (*pulling Jonathan violently down from*

281

chair)I SAID SHUDDUP!!! EVERYBODY!!! (*There is silence. Sidney goes to help Jonathan.*) LEAVE HIM ALONE . .

SIDNEY

Paul . . he's . .

PAUL

Are you gonna go home? GO HOME . . GODDAMNIT, GO HOME . . YOU WANT TO STAY WITH JONATHAN . . YOU'LL NEVER GET HOME . . GO HOME . . JONATHAN . . DO YOU HAVE A JOB???

JONATHAN

Paul . . Let me finish.

PAUL

JONATHAN, DO YOU HAVE A JOB?

JONATHAN

No . . I . .

PAUL

NO . . PETER DO YOU HAVE A JOB?

PETER

No . . I . .

PAUL

THEN WHAT THE HELL ARE YOU TALKING ABOUT . . ALL RIGHT, THEN YOU TAKE 'EM ALL HOME . . EVERYBODY . . YOU TAKE 'EM ALL HOME . .

PETER

Paul, you don't have to shout . .

PAUL

WHY NOT . .

PETER

We hear you . .

PAUL

JONATHAN, DO YOU HEAR ME?

JONATHAN

Paul . . please listen . .

PAUL

DOES EVERYBODY HEAR ME??? YOU CAN ALL GO HOME NOW. THE WAR IS OVER . . YOU CAN GO HOME NOW . . GOOOOOOOOO!!!

JONATHAN

Paul . . look . . look, where am I going to go . .

PAUL

I've been told that's not my problem . . right, Peter?

JONATHAN

Let's go . . Peter . . We'll have a drink . .

PAUL

NOT A DRINK! JONATHAN, FOR CHRIST'S SAKE . . WHEN ARE YOU GOING TO FLY RIGHT??? (*Jonathan starts to get his coat; Sidney and Peter go out the door*) Jonathan? (*Jonathan gets his coat . . starts out*) Jonathan? (*he moves up to the door*) Jonathan? JONATHAN?

JONATHAN

What . .

PAUL

I'm sorry . . (*He breaks down and sobs. Jonathan re-enters. As Paul sobs, he waits. He begins humming, then singing as he moves back to Paul.*)

JONATHAN

Alleluia
Alleluia
Al-le-lu-ia . . Allelulia

Show us, oh Lord, Thy mercy!
And grant us Thy salvation.

PAUL . . (*whispers*) Paul . . (*Paul looks up*) Alleluia . . (*Jonathan leans over, picks up his suitcase, and starts out of the apartment, as off-stage we hear Peter scream*)

PETER

Come on, Jonathan . . I think I know where there's a party . . Party . . Come on. Partyyyyy . . Party time . . Partyyyyyyyyyy. (*Jonathan leaves. As we become aware of the rock and roll record still playing on the machine, the record ends and clicks off. The arm pulls back and the next record drops.*)

JONATHAN'S VOICE

This is a recording . . The following will be one minute of absolute silence. (*Paul lifts his head slowly . . and looks . . as the silence plays on . .)

SLOW CURTAIN